DATE DUE

MAR 0 2 1999	
MAY 1 0 1999	
NOV 1 8 1999	
DEC 0 2 1999	
MAR 0 2 2001	
MAY 0 6 2002	
OCT 2 8 2002	
MAR 2 2 2005	
DEC 1 3 2011	

URT

copyright 1988

Allenby Press, Arcadia, California

TRAFFIC COURT

HOW TO WIN

BY

JAMES A. GLASS
ATTORNEY AT LAW

Published by:
Allenby Press
701 South First Ave. Suite 272
Arcadia, Ca. 91006, U.S.A.

Copyright @ 1988 by James A. Glass
Printed in the United States of America
Library of Congress Cataloging in Publication Data.
Glass, James A., 1942-
  Traffic court : how to win / by James A. Glass.
    p.   cm.
  Includes index
      1. Traffic Court--United States--Popular works.
      2. Traffic violations--United States--Popular works.
        I. Title.
  KF2232.Z9G53 1988
  345.73'0247--dc 19
  [347.305247]   87-21280
                                                  CIP

To my wife Betty without whose encouragement, editing and design this book would not have been possible.

WARNING - DISCLAIMER

This book is designed to provide information only in regard to the subject matter covered. It is sold with the understanding that the publisher and author are not herein engaged in rendering legal or professional services. If legal or other professional advice is required, the services of a competent professional should be sought.

Every effort has been made to make this book as complete and accurate as possible. However, there may be mistakes both typographical and in content. Therefore this text should be used as a general guide to the court system and not as the ultimate legal source. This book contains information on law and court procedures only up to the date of publication. Law and procedures are changed by the courts and legislatures daily and therefore the ultimate sources for such information are the legal publications of the state and county in which you reside. If you act in court without the services of a lawyer you are in actual fact treated as a lawyer and will be held responsible to the same degree as a lawyer licensed to practice law in your state.

Since each case is different, this book is not intended to be, nor can it be, a substitute for the competent professional advice of an attorney. Consult an attorney when needed.

The author and Allenby Press shall have no liability nor responsibility to any person or entity with respect to any loss or damage caused or alleged to be caused directly or indirectly by the information contained in this book.

WARNING - DISCLAIMER

TABLE OF CONTENTS

FIGURES

"WHY ME?"

"YOU HAVE BEEN SELECTED
AS
A REPRESENTATIVE OF YOUR FELLOW
DRIVERS."

(Statement of Traffic Officer to Disgusted Motorist)

CHAPTER ONE

HOW YOU CAN WIN IN TRAFFIC COURT

Are you nervous, frightened, angry, frustrated, impatient, bewildered, confused or all of the above because you have to go to court? These feelings are common to all who go to court, especially the defendant and his witnesses.

These feelings are normal. The basic cause of these feelings is fear of the unknown. This is due to a lack of knowledge of the court system and a lack of confidence in one's ability to handle oneself in court.

Going to court with a lawyer may relieve one's anxiety, but for most people, it is too expensive. For this reason, the use of a lawyer's services is rare in traffic court; except in the more serious jailable traffic offenses and of course, the state's use of a prosecuting attorney. However, consultation with an attorney may be a good idea depending on the case.

"TRAFFIC COURT" can be used as a roadmap to guide you through the courtrooms of the U.S.A.. The traffic court process is explained from arrest to appeal (start to finish) so that you can feel more comfortable and confident in court thus becoming, at the very least, an emotional winner.

Once you know what to expect and how to handle the procedures the whole process of traffic court becomes a lot less threatening. That is the reason for this book—to help you handle yourself in court and to WIN.

Winning in traffic court does not just mean being found not guilty of the offense charged or having the case dismissed, although, of course, that would be ideal.

Winning takes on many appearances.

•You can win in the field by knowing what to expect when pulled over by the officer so that you may be able to avoid the ticket, or avoid being taken to jail.

•If you do not go to court to fight your ticket you have lost automatically. Merely by going to court you have taken a stand which is a winning one.

•By fighting your ticket and going to court you have reduced the profitability of the procedure by costing the city, county and state the necessary money to put on a court proceeding.

•When you appear in court you may be able to get your case dismissed, be found not guilty, have your fine suspended or reduced, avoid a conviction on your driving record, reduce a "point count" and protect your license. These are all WINS.

•Insurance rates will probably go up, your ability to get your driver's license automatically renewed will be affected, points will be added to your driving record which could eventually result in loss of your driving privilege, or subsequent offenses may be elevated into more serious ones as a result of your not fighting back. Therefore you Win if you are able to prevent any of these occurrences.

•You win just by going to court for you have automatically changed the odds that were against you one hundred percent when you simply pay your ticket. That way you can be delighted when you win and shouldn't be bothered when you lose. If enough people would understand what is happening and fight back, the system could be changed.

The basic idea in our criminal justice system is

that the defendant is presumed innocent until proven guilty beyond a reasonable doubt.

What this means is that you cannot be sentenced by the judge until you have plead guilty or have gone to trial and been found guilty.

However, especially in traffic court, the odds are that you are going to plead guilty whether you are guilty or not. Most people are unwilling to take the time to fight a traffic ticket and pay up immediately.

For those of you who are willing to fight back, the odds are changed more in your favor but are still high. Many officers do not consider traffic tickets as a big deal and if they have something better to do will not come to court. In that event you win by getting your case dismissed.

Many prosecutors do not like traffic trials. They are used to handling more important cases. They are therefore willing to deal in the appropriate traffic case. By going to court and asking for such consideration you may get a reduction in charge, a reduction in fine or point court, traffic school, etc., and therefore win.

Winning in trial is still difficult even though you are presumed innocent until proven guilty beyond a reasonable doubt. There are several reasons for this situation.

Most traffic ticket situations are one on one, you against the officer. The officer's job is usually characterized as "traffic enforcement". This means that he is supposed to write tickets. While he has not been given a specific quota of tickets to write you can imagine the reaction at headquarters if he isn't writing enough tickets. In addition, he knows that most of you won't be fighting the ticket. In court, the officer is usually believed. He is a professional witness that has probably testified hundreds of times. Most officers tell what they saw or rather remember seeing happen. But there are some who will "build a case" and fill in the gaps which would leave you innocent. This still amazes this writer but it happens. It leaves a bad taste in everyone's mouth and ruins it for the honest officers.

If the officer has a bad reputation, the court will probably not believe his version of the story if you present a believable defense. However, if you just accuse the officer of lying without presenting appropriate evidence you will still lose.

You are only entitled to a court trial in traffic court in most states. This means that the judge is the only one who hears your case and decides if you are guilty. He hears so many of these cases it is sometimes very hard to listen afresh. An attitude of "if he got the ticket he is probably guilty" can prevail. In addition there are some very real pressures on him to convict as you will shortly see.

We would all protest a doubling of our taxes, wouldn't we? Of course, but not when it slipped in as a fine. In California, for example, there was not a whimper among the people when the legislature doubled the maximum fines for traffic infractions starting in 1985. Of course, the courts immediately started imposing higher fines.

This is a form of taxation in which we, as taxpayers, have little awareness or voice. Traffic courts are therefore in the business of making money, although no law states that as an objective. You can see that there is a great reason and necessity for them to do so. The reason is that the revenue which is collected by the courts by means of fines and forfeited bails is divided up by the cities and counties in which the tickets are written with a sum left over for the state. In addition, to use California as an example, there may be a "penalty assessment" of approximately seventy percent tacked onto the fine which goes entirely to the state. So a maximum fine of $100 is now $170. You can see that it would cost all those financially interested large sums of money if too many people were found not guilty or had their fines suspended.

Such funds are supposed to be used for the support of law enforcement and the courts.

> *This writer has known of situations where the prosecuting attorney wouldn't let a particular judge hear traffic cases because he found too many people not guilty and suspended too many fines. The uproar by the local law enforcement agencies was so loud it forced the prosecutor to take this action.*

Traffic Schools were designed for traffic education and hopefully to prevent the occurrence of traffic violations and accidents. Most courts will allow the case to be dismissed or a point count reduced in return for attending the school. This results in loss of revenues to the courts. Traffic schools are therefore being limited in their use by some courts because they may cost more to administer than the funds that would be raised by convictions and fines. To be fair, there have been many abuses by the traffic schools in not legitimately providing the intended services.

Going to court is extremely inconvenient for most people for numerous reasons such as the time away from work, the necessity for several court appearances, long lines, lack of courtesy, need for baby sitters.

Remember that it takes time and money for the

state to become involved in a traffic trial and cuts down the value of a conviction. Therefore you WIN when you fight your ticket by causing these costs and by so doing you have much more power over what finally happens to your case than if you just give up.

There is, at least, the satisfaction of having tried to do what you could for yourself. Of course, if you are truly guilty of the offense, you may feel better just going ahead and paying the fine. If most people didn't do exactly that the system would break down. You can be assured that the court systems as presently set up are incapable of handling the mess if everyone were to fight their tickets.

This writer still regrets not fighting a ticket he got twenty-five years ago which he still feels was undeserved.

Remember: you are entitled to a trial whether you are guilty or not. The saying of the words, "not guilty" merely sets into action the trial process. It is a Constitutional Right which you have in contrast to most of the people of the world, so don't be ashamed or afraid to use it.

If you keep the above items in mind you can see that, except for convenience there is no reason not to fight back. You have nothing to lose and everything to gain. You WIN by fighting your ticket.

CHAPTER TWO

HOW TO USE "TRAFFIC COURT"

"TRAFFIC COURT" is of universal application throughout the United States. This book is based on interviews of magistrates, prosecutors and public defenders in numerous states, a review of the driver's guides and laws of the various states as well as my seventeen plus years of experience in California courts.

It was found that while there are some slight differences in the laws of each state the basic procedures and tactics are the same.

Most states have enacted a Uniform Traffic Safety Law which accounts for the basic similarities. Because laws change so rapidly this book cannot be considered as a definitive statement of law. For that reason sections of law have not been quoted except as examples. You should use "TRAFFIC COURT" along with a copy of the up to date laws of your state.

"TRAFFIC COURT" is designed to lead you step by step through the procedures of traffic court. After you have read the book you should then refer back to the sections which you find most helpful.

If you have already received a traffic ticket you should immediately try to obtain a copy of the law governing your offense. Be sure you have the right section. Read it carefully. Once you understand the nature of the charge you will be ready to apply the suggestions of "TRAFFIC COURT". If you have difficulty in locating the right books see APPENDIX A—"Law

Books: How To Find And Use Them".

Plan your course of action so that you have an objective in going to traffic court. For example:

•You are going to fight the ticket because you are not guilty of it and therefore want a trial.

•You just want to see if the officer will show up to try to get a dismissal.

•You want to be able to minimize the consequences to yourself by reducing the fine, or lowering your point count to protect your license, etc..

Outline each step you should take for your particular case using "TRAFFIC COURT" as a guide. The outline can then be used as a checklist as you move from one stage in the proceedings to another. The necessary information has been supplied to enable you to prepare such an outline. Since each case is unique you need to do the outline yourself in order to truly prepare yourself for court. Most lawyers will have some form of outline to guide them through their cases until they have developed more experience.

It is common to take a piece of paper and divide it in half lengthwise. On one half you place your outline. You use the other half for note taking. In addition, prepare a time table and calendar all court dates and/or due dates for interviews, hearings, proof of repairs or compliance dates so that you do not miss them. It is very important to be on time and on the right day for court matters otherwise you could end up in jail.

While this book is designed for easy reference and carrying, it is probably not a good idea to use it in the courtroom for reference. The judge would probably think you are using somebody else's material and would stop listening to you. Prepare your own outline and use it.

The words "judge", "commissioner", "referee", "magistrate" and "hearing officer" are used interchangeably. They all are equal to the words "the court". Their specific meanings are explained later. However, if you are standing in front of someone with one of those titles, black robe or not, address her as "Your Honor". That is how you talk to them. For example: "Yes, Your Honor". Go on, it won't hurt. They will all answer to "judge" even if technically they are not judges.

The term "DMV" (Department of Motor Vehicles) is used to refer to all agencies which deal with your driving privilege.

This book is not intended as a substitute for the legal advice or services that can be provided by a lawyer. If you have any questions, consult a lawyer.

By following the above suggestions and the rest of the suggestions in the book you will be able to be confident in yourself and no matter what happens, be a winner in traffic court.

DEFENDANT'S COPY

CITY OF   **CALIFORNIA**

NOTICE TO APPEAR   P 283311

DATE	TIME		DAY OF WEEK	SHIFT	AREA
19					

NAME (FIRST, MIDDLE, LAST)

RESIDENCE ADDRESS	CITY/ZIP

BUSINESS ADDRESS	CITY/ZIP

DRIVER'S LICENSE NO.	STATE	CLASS	AGE	BIRTHDATE	JUV.

SEX	RACE	HAIR	EYES	HEIGHT	WEIGHT
M F					

VEHICLE LICENSE NO.	STATE	PASSENGERS
		M F

VEHICLE YEAR	MAKE	MODEL	BODY STYLE	COLOR

REGISTERED OWNER OR LESSEE	☐ SAME AS ABOVE

ADDRESS OF OWNER OR LESSEE	☐ SAME AS ABOVE

Items checked are cited in accordance
with 40610(b) CVC—See reverse

☐ BOOKING REQUIRED   CASE NO.

☐	VIOLATION(S)	CODE	SECTION	DESCRIPTION
☐				
☐				
☐				

	SPEED			RADAR	INVOLVED IN ACCIDENT
APPROX	PF/MAX	VEH LMT	SAFE		☐

DIRECTION OF TRAVEL
N S E W

☐
☐ OR _____ FEET **N S E W** OF _____ (STREET OR HIGHWAY)

(STREET OR HIGHWAY)

	WEATHER				TRAFFIC		
☐ DRY	☐ WET	☐ FOG		☐ HEAVY	☐ MEDIUM	☐ LIGHT

COMMENTS:

☐   OFFENSE(S) NOT COMMITTED IN MY PRESENCE. CERTIFIED ON INFORMATION AND BELIEF
I CERTIFY UNDER PENALTY OF PERJURY THAT THE FOREGOING IS TRUE AND CORRECT.
EXECUTED ON THE DATE SHOWN ABOVE AT _____ , CALIFORNIA

ISSUING OFFICER	I.D. NO.	DAYS OFF

NAME OF ARRESTING OFFICER-IF DIFFERENT FROM ABOVE	I.D. NO.	DAYS OFF

WITHOUT ADMITTING GUILT, I PROMISE TO APPEAR AT THE TIME AND PLACE CHECKED BELOW.

X SIGNATURE

BEFORE A JUDGE OR A CLERK OF THE MUNICIPAL COURT

☐ MUNICIPAL COURT OF

☐ JUVENILE COURT - TRAFFIC DIVISION,
   (JUVENILES MUST BE ACCOMPANIED BY PARENTS)

☐ _____ BLVD. _____ CALIF.

☐ COUNTY _____ CALIF.

on the _____ day of _____ , 19 _____ at 8:00 a.m. ☐
                                                  6:00 p.m. ☐

FORM APPROVED BY THE
JUDICIAL COUNCIL OF CALIFORNIA PPD-30   OTHER _____
REV. 6/84 V.C. 40500(B) P.C. 853.9

SEE REVERSE SIDE

TRAFFIC TICKET

FIGURE 1

CHAPTER THREE

GETTING THE TICKET

The flashing lights pull behind you. You say, "Why me? What did I do? What do I do now?

Pull over as quickly and safely as possible. Do not keep going in the hope that he really doesn't mean you. A quick, safe pullover means you were alert. After all how could you have committed the alleged violations if you responded so rapidly? Continuing to drive for a time before pulling over, especially if the officer has to use his siren, means you were inattentive. Pull over to the far right as it is safer and will be appreciated. If you try to get away from the officer you will be committing a more serious crime called evading arrest. You will probably be taken to jail instead of being released in the field with a traffic ticket.

Don't make any sudden movements, particularly at night. Many officers have been killed or injured during traffic stops so they are very careful, so you be careful too. Keep your hands in sight and don't start rummaging under your seat or in the glove box. If you are trying to hide something, don't try. It is surprising how much the officer can see from behind you even at night.

Don't you or your passengers throw anything from the car. If you have something to hide it is too late to do it when the officer is behind you. Sit still and pray. If you have been drinking or smoking opening the windows while still moving may help flush out the odor but don't count on it.

Keep your passengers under control and quiet.

You don't need a peanut gallery. Their actions or statements could get you a ticket and them arrested. The best course of action for everyone is to be quiet, calm and still. If questioned, be polite.

Remember that you may be legally responsible for the actions of your passengers in many cases such as their wearing seat belts, drinking in the car or bringing open containers of alcohol into the car as well as permitting the use of any illegal drugs.

It is safer and wiser to remain seated unless instructed by the officer to get out. If you get out of your vehicle hoping that the officer won't look into it, you are mistaken—he will. Remember that an officer is trained to look for law violations. The traffic stop only gives him another chance to look for other violations. If he sees some kind of violation he will act on it. He will be looking for drugs, open containers of alcohol, weapons or contraband.

If you get out of the car voluntarily he will be able to notice your balance and attire, checking for intoxication. He may be given a reason to conduct a "pat down" search; that is, go over the exterior of your body in a search for weapons. He will say it is for "officer safety". Also, by staying in the car you are staying with your witnesses and not separating yourself from them.

Wait to be asked to get out your driver's license and open your window. You know you are going to be asked and by doing it first you may create a good impression. You are licensed aren't you? However, it is better to keep you hands in sight and not to fidget around for as mentioned before this makes officers nervous. Your license will be the first thing the officer will ask for and next will be the registration of the vehicle. Always keep both your license and registration in easy to get to places. Remove your license from your wallet. Don't try to hand your wallet to the officer, he probably won't take it. He doesn't want to take the chance of being accused of taking something from you wallet and you do not want to be accused of bribery. There are some areas of the country where the practice of slipping a bill behind your license and giving it to the officer is followed. This is obviously bribery and you are taking an extreme chance on doing it. It is a practice to avoid. Bribery is a felony in most states and a lot more serious than a traffic ticket.

The most important advice to follow is—Stay calm, cool, polite, and quiet. A good attitude is the best tool you have in avoiding a ticket. This is especially important if you are a minor. Do not get wise. Avoid showing off for your friends. The officer is a human being just like everyone else and like most adults won't like smart kids or smart mouths. If you are close to a school, college, or in a college town, or on a holiday where there are many other young people, the only thing you may have going for you is an exceptionally good attitude. Remember that statements you make can and will be used against you in court. You will not be warned or told of your constitutional right to be silent. "Yes Sir", "No Sir", can work wonders. It may mean the difference between the officer writing the ticket or not. A loud mouth buys trouble. Do not bluster, cry, or threaten. You are often asked if you know why you are being stopped. Answer, "No". You really don't know for sure. When he tells you why you were stopped, answer using a noncommittal, "Oh". Neither outraged indignation nor an admission of guilt is wise. The less you say is usually better.

If you are going to try to talk yourself out of

the ticket be polite and respectful. Do not give excuses, unless they are really good ones that can be backed up, as the officer has probably heard them all. You might try asking a question such as "Would you tell me exactly what I did wrong?" or "How can I repair my car so I don't get stopped again?", "I didn't realize I was going that fast, could you give me a warning?" or "This is my first offense (in years), could you give me a chance?" (Remember that he is going to run a records check on you.)

The officer will ask you questions regarding your identification; that is, name, address, date of birth, who is the registered owner of the vehicle, etc.. You should answer truthfully. Giving false information to a police officer is a serious offense. If you know, or suspect, that you have warrants out for your arrest, accept what happens. Lying will only get you into deeper trouble.

If he asks questions about your driving, don't answer except in a very noncommittal way, as mentioned before. You can say, "I do not wish to talk about it". *Remember, silence cannot be used against you while your statements can.* If you have been drinking or using some other form of intoxicant you especially shouldn't try to talk your way out of it. The fact is that if the officer has enough information to arrest or ticket you, he will. You should not help him. If you are stopped at dawn, dusk or night, you will find yourself looking at the officer's flashlight. This is shined into your face to observe the reactions of your pupils as an indication of intoxication. If you have already adjusted your pupils by looking at a street or car light there probably will not be much reaction.

Cooperate if the officer asks you to get out of the car. If he asks to search the car you may refuse. (See below.) He may detain you for a short time, without your permission, while he has you and your car checked for "wants and warrants"; that is, to see if the car is stolen and if you have any warrants out for your arrest. You have paid your fines on other tickets haven't you? If not, you are going to be arrested. (See Chapter 15—Arrest and Release.)

The key to avoiding being arrested and taken to jail instead of getting a traffic ticket is for you and your passenger(s) to be cooperative. If it appears that the officer is going to take you to jail remain cooperative. You will probably have to be handcuffed. Even if you think this is outrageous stay calm. This is a common practice in almost every case, male or female. Besides, handcuffs are very uncomfortable and depending on how the officer puts them on can really hurt. If they feel too tight, you can ask the officer, politely, to loosen them. Resisting the officer's actions or interfering with them will escalate your moving violation and/ or arrest for a warrant into the new crime of resisting arrest or interfering with a police officer. You may and should refuse a request to search and refuse to answer questions, other than those relating to personal identification. If you feel that the officer is out of line in his treatment of you, you may file a complaint with his department. The complaints are always checked out. Do not threaten him. The less you say the better.

Do not challenge the officer. Do not call him names, be disrespectful or tell him that he can't give you a ticket. Do not threaten him with lawsuits or complaints to his superiors or that "you'll see him in court". These actions will guarantee that not only will you get a ticket and that it will cover as many violations as the officer can think of but that he will be sure to remember you and most definitely appear in court for your trial.

You should remember that the officer has no right to search the car unless he has a search warrant or your actions give him what is known as "probable cause" to search. That is, enough facts that if he asked a judge for a warrant he could get one. One example is a "dipping shoulder"which means a "furtive gesture"; that is, you are trying to hide something. Another example is his seeing an open container of beer. If you give permission then he can go ahead and search. He usually doesn't have to tell you that you do not have to allow the search. It is amazing how many people forget what they have in their cars. You may ask yourself why not agree? After all you have nothing to hide.—SO WHAT!—Your right against unlawful search and seizure is constitutionally guaranteed. Why should you or your property be searched is the question to ask. If he does search after your refusal do not fight him or try to stop him, you will simply get into more trouble.

Sign the ticket after reading it. Your signature is merely a promise to appear in court. It is not an admission of guilt. If you refuse to sign the ticket you will be arrested and taken to jail. A traffic ticket is an alternative to being arrested and having to post cash bail or a bail bond.

You may, before signing the ticket, request that your case be heard at the county seat. You must check your vehicle code to see if this is possible. This may get you a court house closer to where you live as well as discourage the officer from appearing if it is farther from his regular patrol area. If refused note it on the ticket and then sign it.

If you are from out of state, or live too far from where you will have to appear, you can refuse to sign the ticket. This will result in your being taken directly to the court, if open (it could be the jail) where you can either pay the fine or post a forfeitable bail. This could be dangerous as he might not let you drive your car. Instead, your car could be left or impounded. You could be handcuffed, booked, searched and jailed before you get a chance to pay. Better yet ask the officer if you can have a hearing or go to pay the ticket that day without the above problems. If he says no, then sign the ticket.

Observe your surroundings if you intend to fight the citation. Depending upon the ticket, various conditions of the area and your vehicle will be important. Things to check are: speedometer, lights, wipers, license plate light, registration tags, condition of vehicle, time of day, weather, traffic, pedestrians, condition of road, amount of traffic, location of traffic signs, street lighting and other lighting conditions and possible witnesses.

After you find out what you are being cited for the above observations can be narrowed down. As soon as possible after receiving the ticket be sure that you write down your version of what happened along with the time and date. Also, get your witnesses to prepare an independent statement and sign it along with the date and the time. The police do this so why not you?

If the appearance of the location where the officer says the incident occurred is important take notes and photos of the location as soon as possible after receiving the ticket. These may be used in court.

Obviously, the best way to avoid getting a ticket is to obey the law and drive safely. Also, be sure your vehicle is kept in good mechanical order. The appearance of the exterior of your car can be very important.

Be sure you have all the necessary lights and that they are working. Be sure that you have the required number of license plates. Most states require both a front and rear license plate and that they be visible. The light to your rear license plate should be working. Check that your registration is up to date and that you have put any necessary stickers in the appropriate places. Remember, that you are responsible for the condition of the car regardless of who owns it.

Do not overload the car either with material or people. If you are towing be sure that you meet the tow requirement of the state as well as the weight requirements.

You cannot guard against an unexpected burnt out light or equipment malfunction, but once they have been called to your attention fix them.

It is recommended in all the drivers' education classes that before starting to drive any car you conduct a walk around inspection and check the above items. Most of us do not do this but it is a good idea. It can save us from both ticket and accident grief latter.

Also realize that your choice of car can result in your getting more attention from the officer. Police officers will watch sports cars more closely than a four door sedan. They will pay more attention to jalopies, low riders, and junk cars than to your small grey hatchback. You may not be able to do anything about this except be aware and watch your driving.

One final point in avoiding trouble, do not do favors for a friend by driving an obviously defective car or loaning one. If you have been drinking and a friend is too drunk to drive do not do it for him. Call a cab or get some other form of transportation.

CHAPTER FOUR

APPEARANCES AND PENALTIES

The type of offense or crime will determine if you must appear in court or whether you can post bail and forfeit it, if you wish. By forfeiting the bail you are in effect pleading guilty, being sentenced and paying the penalty without going to court.

The maximum and minimum penalties for each offense are specified by legislation with the judge being given discretion to suspend or impose whatever penalty he feels is appropriate. The only exception to this is where there are specified minimum penalties which must be imposed regardless of the individual circumstances.

Crimes are classified by their penalties. Each state has different classes of these offenses. There may be infractions or petty misdemeanors; or first, second or third degree misdemeanors; as well as first, second or third degree felonies. That is why it is important to check your local law to find out the possibilities. Infractions or petty misdemeanors carry a fine and usually no jail penalty. A misdemeanor carries a fine and/or a county jail sentence. Felonies carry fines and/or state prison sentences. Some felonies are alternative sentence crimes which means they may be filed as or reduced to misdemeanors by either the prosecuting attorney or the judge.

For example, in California as of 1987, an infraction had a maximum fine of $100 for a first offense. A misdemeanor, unless otherwise defined, had a maximum penalty of six months in jail and/or a $500 fine. A felony had a maximum sentence of three years in the state prison and a $1000 fine unless otherwise specified. Some crimes carry very specific penalties and these penalties will be listed with the specific crimes. Some states, like Utah, have their vehicle code violations as a part of the penal code and there are possible jail sentences for offenses which would not be jailable in other states.

> *This writer was assured by one court clerk in Utah that no one was ever jailed for a minor traffic violation, but...*

Mandatory court appearances are required for misdemeanors and felonies and for certain infractions such as driving faster than the maximum speed limit. When you are given the citation you will be told whether you are required to appear. It will also be written on the citation.

Most non moving violations such as parking, registration or equipment violations do not require a court appearance. You will be told, by the officer and by the citation what steps you have to take to avoid having to appear in court. Usually, you can pay by mail or have the ticket certified to show that you are now in compliance and mail it in to the court. Always make a copy of anything that you send to court and send it at least certified mail, return receipt requested.

Most moving violations which are classed as infractions or petty misdemeanors do not require a court appearance.

What all this means is that for an infraction which does not require a court appearance you can post a "bail", which is really a fine, and not appear in court on the date specified on your citation without a warrant being issued for your arrest. Instead the bail will be forfeited; that is, used for the fine. This is treated as a conviction and goes on your driving record.

In the case of an equipment violation or lack of registration for your vehicle, you may, in many instances, get the item fixed and by showing proof of correction to the appropriate agency get the ticket "signed off". Then by sending in that "proof of correction" you not only do not have to appear but you may not have to pay any bail or fine.

Your driving record will show all violations except equipment and registration violations. This information is easily obtained by anyone with access to your driver's license number. This is for the use of law enforcement and obviously insurance companies. Now you know why they want your driver's license number on your insurance applications.

Most violations are kept on your record for at least three years except for Driving Under the Influence convictions which are kept at least five years (seven years in California) and other priorable convictions. In actual practice, I have found that nothing is removed from your record.

The keeping of the record for this period of time is done for several reasons:

•**Point Counts.** This is where the law assigns a certain number of points to each moving violation and totals them. If you accumulate too many points then your driver's license will be suspended or revoked. In California, for example, each moving violation is considered one point. Driving Under the Influence, Reckless Driving, Speed Contest and Hit and Run are assigned two points. Then if you accumulate four points in one year, six points in two years or eight points in three years, your privilege to drive can be suspended. More often, you will be placed on a form of probation the first time. Other states assign different points per violation. These are usually listed in your driver's license study guide and, of course, your state law books.

•**Priors.** This term means that many offenses, such as speeding convictions, can be added up so that if you get too many convictions they can be moved up from an infraction to a misdemeanor, which carries a possible jail sentence. In Driving Under the Influence cases, the maximum and minimum penalties are increased and the discretion of the judge in sentencing you is increasingly limited. For instance, in California for a first offense DUI there is a minimum forty-eight hours in jail which can be suspended with a license restriction. A second offense within seven years will require the forty-eight hours in jail and other penalties and a third offense DUI within seven years will require a mandatory minimum jail sentence of four months plus a minimum fine of about $690 and a mandatory alcohol treatment program. Maximum sentence is one year in jail.

•**Sentencing**. When the judge is going to sentence you she looks at your "rap sheet" which is the computer printout of your driving record. She will take the number of offenses shown into consideration in determining the penalty.

•**Insurance.** An insurance company can look at your record and use it to decide if they will issue or cancel a policy and what your rate will be.

There are a few things that you can do about avoiding or minimizing this driving record:

•**Drive defensively and legally to avoid the ticket in the first place.**

•**Fight Back**. If you fight your ticket and win, it cannot be used against you. Although, in the case of misdemeanors or felonies, the arrest will show followed by a statement of case dismissed, or not guilty.

In some states, like California, the judge may order the offense removed from your record following acquittal if he feels that you were "factually innocent". A finding of not guilty is not equivalent to a finding of factually innocent. "Factually innocent" means not only that the judge had to find you not guilty because of a reasonable doubt as to guilt but that she had no doubt. You must ask the judge to make such a order after being acquitted. It does not happen automatically.

•**Traffic School**, if available, will allow you to prevent the offense from going on your record or may be used to reduce your point count to help save your license. You may request traffic school from either the clerk or the judge when you first go to court. (See Chapter 6—Arraignment.)

•**Expungement of the the conviction**. This means that once you have been sentenced and thereafter finished your sentence and/or probationary period, you may apply to the court to have your conviction set aside, a plea of not guilty entered and the case dismissed. This will not remove the offense from the record but will prevent its being used against you. This act is limited by the law with specific exclusions. For example, an offense like Driving Under the Influence may be expunged from your record for the purpose of insurance applications but is still usable by the courts and the DMV for increasing the penalties for subsequent offenses.

If expungement is available, you must check the law to see if it applies to you. The court may be theoretically responsible for telling you of the availability of the remedy but in practice they rarely do tell you. So look it up. (In California, it is sections 1203.4 and 1203.5 of the Penal Code.)

•**Nullify the arrest**. If you have been arrested and released with no charges being filed you may be able to get a statement from the police which should also be entered in the record that you were "detained only, deemed not an arrest". This should prevent its use against you in the future. If the police don't tell you of this, ask. If refused and no charges are filed later after your release you may ask the court for such an order. Again, you must look up the specific law. This does not apply if you are cited or arrested and must either forfeit your bail or go to court.

CHAPTER FIVE

PRACTICE RUN

Preparing ahead of time will make going to court less nerve wracking. Each of the following suggestions should be carried out before you actually have to go to court so that on the real "D" day you will be familiar with the territory and be free to concentrate on the matters at hand.

•Make sure you have written down the court date and time in several locations. "Forgetting" to go to court can be disastrous. Being late can be about as bad, as judges really dislike people being late and have been known to put them in jail. It does not matter if the judge is late.

•Make sure you know the location of the court house and how to get there. The address will be on your ticket.

•Be sure that you have your ticket in a safe place and write down its number, which is usually located in the upper right hand corner of the ticket (see Figure 1), in the same place as you put the date and time of your appearance. In case the ticket is misplaced at least you will have the number which will be needed when you actually go to court. It is a good idea to make a photocopy of your ticket as sometimes you are required to give the original to the clerk of the court. This way you will have a copy to refer to in court.

•Make the necessary arrangements with your work and/or baby sitter.

•Night court may be available. Check the ticket for the date and time of night court as it is probably different from the daytime appearance.

•Check your car or travel arrangements to be sure that they are working on "D" Day.

•Look over your original written statement. If you haven't written down what happened, do it now.

•Make sure you have had your photographs developed.   If you intend to use charts or diagrams now is the time to prepare them (more later in Chapter Eight—Pretrial).   You will not be using these items until the day of trial.   The reason for making sure these items are prepared so far ahead of time is to enable you to prepare more easily for the rest of the trial process.

•Practice making your statement in front of the mirror and a friend. What you say will depend upon what you have decided to do about your ticket (see Chapter Seven—Arraignment).

•Go to the courthouse ahead of time.   Locate the parking. Find out where you can park the longest. Be prepared to be at court at least the entire morning on the day of arraignment and longer on the day of trial. Go inside and locate the restroom (you'll need it). Find the clerk's office and the traffic window. You will probably go there first on the actual court day. Locate the court room and go inside to see what it looks like (see Figure 2).

If you can't get away to go to court ahead of time be sure to get there as early as possible on your court date. You can be sure there will be a long line and you need time to get through the line and get familiar with the courthouse.

•Watch a few traffic arraignments and trials.

This will give you an idea of what to expect. See what impression the judge makes on you. You may not want to have that particular judge hear your case (see Chapter Six—Arraignments).

•Dress appropriately. *Of all the suggestions mentioned this is one of the most important.* You will have only a few minutes to convey a message to the judge from the time you enter the court room. For this reason it is wise to dress so that you don't stand out. You don't want to be the best or the worst dressed person in court. That is why a practice run is helpful as it can give you an idea of how the other people in court are dressed.

Judges are usually conservative in outlook. If you appear and/or are dressed in a radical manner it may have a damaging affect on your case. Therefore: if you are messy, clean up; tattooed, cover up; leave your gang uniform at home; if male and wearing earrings or flashy jewelry, take them off. If you have long and/or messy hair get it cut or at least cleaned up and worn neatly. You do not need to wear a suit or coat and tie but a clean shirt won't hurt. If female, dress neatly and ladylike. The latest look in fashion is not the one to wear to court. Poor doesn't hurt, radical does. If you are a member of the military, wearing your uniform will not hurt.

> *This writer has had to give money to some clients for a quick haircut so the judge wouldn't throw them in jail.*

You may not like these suggestions or may even find them offensive but they are given in order to prepare you for what you are really facing in court.

It does not hurt to remind the judge, by your appearance, that you are a voter.

Finally: Go home and RELAX.

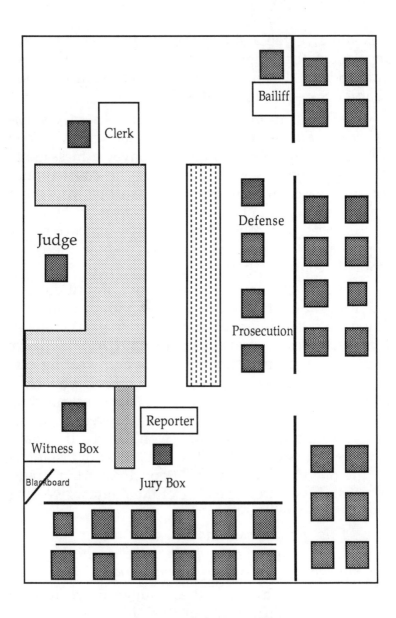

COURTROOOM

FIGURE 2

CHAPTER SIX

ARRAIGNMENT

Your first appearance in court is called an "Arraignment". It is when you are advised of your constitutional rights, the actual charges, and when you enter your plea.

Don't be late. On your ticket will be the date, time and location of your court appearance. Forgetting any one of these can be disastrous. An often heard term is *Failure to Appear*. This means that you either did not appear in court when you were supposed to do so or were too late for your case to be heard. If you miss an appearance or are late a warrant for your arrest will be issued. This is called a "bench warrant" and bail will be set. This means that if you get to court late, after your name has been called, usually twice (referred to as "second call"), you may be taken into custody, searched and locked up.

It is common for a judge to release you if satisfied with your attitude and explanation. This may be after he talks with you or at the end of the court day. However, he may require the posting of bail for future appearances. So DON'T BE LATE.

If you find that you are going to be late, call the court and explain the problem.

When you call the court ask the courthouse telephone operator for the clerk of the traffic court. When you are connected the clerk will usually give you his name, if not, ask for it. Remember it and write it down. If questioned later you will be able to have the fact of your phone call verified. Explain that you will be late, why, and when you will be able to get to the court. Then follow the instructions that you will be given. If the clerk asks you when you can come in, do not tell him you do not know! That attitude, when told to the judge, will get a warrant immediately issued for your arrest.

Remember that when you do not appear the judge must order a warrant for your arrest in order to keep jurisdiction of the case. This is called a "bench warrant". But she does not have to issue it; that is, give the warrant to the police to arrest you. The warrant can be "held" until you appear. Then set aside. This action will prevent any police agency or the court bailiffs from being able to arrest you. The warrant will only be "held"; that is, not issued, if you call in with a reasonable explanation and give a reasonable date when you can make it to court.

If you forget the date, check with the traffic clerk to find out what your date is or was. That is why it is so important not to misplace your ticket and to make the practice run. Go to court as soon as possible. Go to the traffic clerk's office, give them your name, your ticket or its number (remember you kept it safe) and tell them that you missed the day. They will have the case and you sent into court. When the judge calls your name you will be given a chance to explain what happened. Remember, the judge is referred to as "Your Honor".

Be honest. The judge will probably excuse your failure to appear, especially if your appearance is very close to the actual date and withdraw the warrant that has been issued. However, he could fine you for your failure to appear and he could lock you up. Usually, if you walk in, you will walk out. It doesn't hurt to bring some money with you. You can check with the traffic clerk before you come to court to find out the amount of the actual bail so you know how much money to bring with you.

If you just let the ticket be "forgotten" you are subject to arrest. If arrested you will not be released without bail as you were when you first got your ticket. If you don't have the bail money you will remain in jail until you are brought to court.

Actually, in most states, the failure to appear on a written promise to appear (a citation or ticket) is a separate crime which could subject you to up to six months in jail (see Chapter 14—Other Crimes).

An attorney may appear at these court appearances in your absence if he has been hired (retained) by you and authorized to appear for you. If missing work is too costly and you still want to fight your ticket you can hire an attorney.

Get To Court Early!

•On your practice run you will have located the traffic clerk's office. It is the window which has the longest line in front of it.   If you have not gone on a practice run you can plan to use this day as previously suggested in Chapter 5 as long as you get there early.

•Leave your children. They will distract you and cause irritation to the court. They will not get you any sympathy.

•Bring your ticket. You will need it to show to the clerk so your case can be located and sent to court. (It is a good idea to write the number of the citation, usually located at the top right of the ticket in bold face print, and the name of the police agency in some safe place in case you lose the ticket.) The filing system many courts are awful so you must be prepare help yourself as much as possible.

•Bring cash or a "good check". Some courts will accept credit cards. You may decide to pay the ticket or be required to post bail if you request a trial.

•Dress neatly. This topic is repeated for emphasis. Your appearance is one of the most important things over which you have control. Remember that most courts are very conservative. This is not the place for strange or unusual garb. You don't wish to appear wealthy for that may cause an unconscious resentment. If poor, dress as neatly as possible and you will gain respect. Otherwise dress neatly and conservatively. Leave your gang uniform behind. If you are tattooed cover up as much as possible. The judge will regard wild, long hair with contempt. You do not wish to be remembered because of your dress. If you dress too well you may not get any break on the fines. If you are sloppy and dirty, you will probably get no respect and find it difficult to get much help.

•Politeness and a smile works wonders. Most of the clerks are harassed and overworked and really appreciate such courtesy, as do all the court personnel. The reverse is true. If you are really nasty or overbearing you may find yourself ignored, harassed or even arrested.

Some states have a procedure by which you can request a trial date by mail. This information will usually be contained on the citation. If not, call the court and ask what procedure to follow. Great caution is recommended in using and relying on the U.S. Mail. Be sure to use at least certified mail with return receipt requested. If you do not get confirmation of your letter call to verify that it got there.

There is also, in some states, a procedure by which you can have your trial by mail, usually if you live more than one hundred miles from the nearest ⌐ourt. As this is the same, in this writer's opinion, as pleading guilty it is not recommended, except in the case of parking tickets. If you want to fight your ticket you have to be prepared and actually go to court. For details, check with your local court.

When you get to court go to the traffic clerk's office and show them your ticket. The clerk will, usually, ask you if you want to pay the ticket, go to traffic school, or if you want a trial. In some courts the traffic clerk can make all of the above arrangements including setting a trial date. However, other courts will require an actual appearance before the judge. You can find out this information by a phone call to the traffic clerk before coming to court. Call in the middle morning or afternoon as early morning or early afternoon is extremely busy.

If you are going into court use the restroom if needed before the court is called to order. Then have a seat in the courtroom and wait until your name is called.

Once the court is called to order a common procedure is usually followed. It basically consists of: a verbal advisement of your constitutional rights by the judge or a clerk. The use of a tape recorded statement is common or you may be given a written statement of your rights to read and sign; the cases being called to see who is present; the entry of pleas and other court business. The judge hates to repeat himself which is why it is so important to be on time.

The statement of constitutional rights which will be given will apply to you as well as other defendants charged with more serious crimes. You will be told the following:

• *You have the right to a trial before a judge,* commonly called a court trial. Traffic cases are not heard by jury, in most cases. (Don't waste your time by asking for a jury trial. They are only available if there is a possibility of your going to jail.)

• *You are entitled to confront and question (cross-examine) the witnesses against you*: that is, to actually have the witness or witnesses be in court so you can face them and question them.

• *You may have witnesses on your own behalf brought to court* by the subpoena process (a court order) and testify for you.

• *You have the right to be represented by a lawyer of your own choosing*. You are not entitled to appointed counsel even if you are indigent; that is, without funds to hire an attorney.

An indigent person is only entitled to appointed counsel (public defender) if faced with the possibility of a jail sentence. Traffic violations are usually classified as infractions or petty misdemeanors wherein only fines or charitable service can be imposed therefore there is no right to an appointed attorney. However, if you commit the separate crime of failing to appear on your citation, which is a misdemeanor punishable by a jail sentence, you are entitled to appointed counsel if you are indigent (see Chapter 14).

• *You have a right against self-incrimination:* that is, the right to remain silent. You cannot be forced to say anything which can be used against you or to be a witness against yourself. In fact, if you remain silent when the judge asks you how you plead— guilty or not guilty, he will enter a not guilty plea on your behalf. This is not a common occurrence.

• *You have the right to a speedy and public trial:* The judge will tell you that the trial must be within a certain number of days or the case will be dismissed, unless you have either requested or agreed to a date beyond that time limit. For example, in California you must be brought to trial within forty-five days from the date of the arraignment if you are not in custody and thirty days if you are in custody at the time of the arraignment.

After the statement of constitutional rights the judge will generally inform you of the *maximum and minimum penalties* which are provided by the law.

He will also inform you of what pleas are available—usually *guilty, no contest, or not guilty.* He will probably also inform you if *traffic school* is available for certain offenses.

PAY ATTENTION AND LISTEN! These advisements may be given so rapidly and quietly or mumbled that they are difficult to understand (many judges are bored with having to repeat these rights and resent having to give them so they will try to get them over as quickly as possible). If you didn't understand something you may ask for a explanation when your name is called. WARNING: Many judges don't like to be questioned, so pay attention.

Calendar Call will follow the advisement of rights. The judge will call roll to see who is there. Answer loudly and clearly when your name is called. You may be required to come forward at that time or he may wait until they know who is present before calling each individual case. Where there are a great number of defendants, the judge may call more than one person at a time to come forward.

When your name is called you will go from the audience to stand in front of the judge's bench at the counsel table (see Figure 2). The judge will ask you if you are the person called and ask you how you plead. He may ask each individual how he wishes to plead. Then, if he feels that a particular case will take too long, he may have that person sit down and wait until he is through with the easier cases.

There are three pleas which you may enter: Not Guilty, Guilty and No Contest. You may also request Traffic School. If you do not wish to enter a plea at this specific time you may ask for a continuance of the arraignment (a different date) in order to enter a plea at that time.

A Not Guilty plea may be entered whether you are guilty or not because, as you have just been informed by the court, you are constitutionally entitled to a trial. So if you wish a trial for whatever reason answer "Not Guilty". The judge will then set a day and time for the trial and set bail. If that day or time is not convenient you may ask for a different time and/ or date. Be careful here. You are entitled to a speedy trial. If you request a date which takes you beyond that time you will be giving up your right to such speedy trial. If you are counting on the officer not showing up and getting the case dismissed it may not not happen because you have given up the right to a speedy trial and the "people" (prosecution) are entitled to a continuance.

Bail in the amount of the expected fine is set. Therefore if you do not appear at the trial for any reason the bail can be forfeited: that is, surrendered to the court without the necessity for a warrant for your arrest being issued. If you don't have any money or enough money to put up for bail you may ask for a release on your "Own Recognizance" or "O.R." This is a release without bail on your promise to appear similar to when you signed the citation. However, if you fail to appear a warrant will be issued for your arrest as there is no bail to be forfeited, and when caught by the police you will be locked up.

You may ask the judge for an "indicated sen-

tence". He will usually tell you what the fine will be. If you do not like the indicated sentence then you may enter a not guilty plea as above. Otherwise you may enter a guilty plea. A "Guilty" plea gives up all of the rights which you were advised you have, for this case only, and gives the judge the power to sentence you. If he indicated a sentence he will give that sentence.

"Guilty with explanation" is not a legal plea. However, if you say that phrase the judge will usually listen to you before imposing the sentence. You do have a right to be heard before being sentenced as to why you think he should impose a lighter sentence than usual: for example; your speedometer was defective and you have had it fixed or you were taking your child to the doctor.

You want to be careful that you don't talk him into a stiffer sentence. The better procedure in all matters is to keep quiet. Always try out your explanation on a friend before you try it on the judge. If your friend says forget it, give it up.

Guilty as well as No Contest pleas may be entered at any time before the actual trial begins.

"No Contest" is a plea that is treated the same as a Guilty plea. However, the plea may not be used against you in a civil case. This means that if you are involved in a accident which is the basis for your citation and you are sued, the people suing you would have to prove their entire case instead of being able to use your guilty plea as proof of liability. This plea is NOT available at the end of a trial. The judge will either find you "Not Guilty" or "Guilty". If you are found "Guilty" and are then sued the guilty verdict may be used to prove the case against you. This is why, in many cases, you should enter a "No Contest" plea and pay the fine even though you feel that you are "Not Guilty". If there is the slightest question of civil liability, consult a lawyer for advice before going to court. Civil law suits may not be filed until several years after the incident, so it pays to be careful.

"No Contest" may also be used if you do not wish to fight the case, for whatever reason but can't bring yourself to say guilty. It is still treated as a guilty plea.

Traffic School is an alternative offered by some jurisdictions. When you request traffic school you will be asked if you have been to traffic school before. Don't lie. If you are caught you could be put in jail for contempt of court. If you are eligible you will be given a list of approved schools and a date to return to court with proof of completion. This proof is given to you by the traffic school. They will also notify the court if you don't complete the school. Presenting proof of completion will result in dismissal of the case or will prevent your point count on your driving record from being increased (see Chapter 17). You are only allowed one time at traffic school within the year. If you don't complete the school you will be required to go to court and explain why and unless your reason for missing was really good you will not be allowed to make it up. You will be required to proceed with the case by either pleading guilty or going to trial.

A change of plea from "Not Guilty" to "Guilty" or "No Contest" may be done at any time after the entry of the "Not Guilty" plea. A "No Contest" plea may not be entered after a verdict of "Guilty" has been reached after a trial.

However, once you have been sentenced, after a plea, you usually cannot change your plea back to not guilty and request a trial. This will only be allowed if you can show some impropriety occurred or you were mislead into entering the guilty or no contest plea. If you change your mind before sentence is imposed, the judge will be more likely to allow such change of plea.

A "Stipulation" is an agreement between you and the prosecution as to some fact. If you are appearing before a commissioner, referee, hearing officer, or judge "pro tem" (temporary judge) you will be given a "stipulation" to sign. This is an agreement that you will allow that particular person to sit as a judge and hear your case. This individual is a lawyer, in most cases, who has been appointed by the judge or judges of the area to help out.

You are entitled to have your case heard by a judge. Therefore, if for any reason you don't like this individual, don't sign the paper. You should have a good reason for refusing as most judges are busy and resent having to hear a traffic case when they have made arrangements for others to hear them. A refusal to stipulate is usually only important if you are going to plead guilty or no contest and do not want that particular person to sentence you. This applies to trial as well. You may not mind that person doing the arraignment but don't want him to hear your trial.

It is very important to read anything you are given to sign, whether in court or elsewhere. In California, for example, a commissioner can hear arraignments if ordered to do so by the presiding judge without a stipulation being signed by you. However, he cannot sentence you without that signed stipulation.

An "Affidavit of Prejudice" is the name of an oral or written statement which you make if you don't wish to have a particular judge hear your case. You are only allowed one of these challenges. It allows you to prevent a specific judge from hearing your case without your stating a reason. You must file this affidavit before the judge hears your case. It may be oral in some states and other require a writing (see Figure 11). You can ask at the clerk's office ahead of time as to what form is required. Be careful when you do this. Other judges don't much like to have to do the work of the judge being disqualified. However, sometimes it is very necessary.

If, after you have filed an affidavit of prejudice, you find yourself in front of someone else who is really terrible; you may still have a course of action, other than prayer, left. This is called an **"Affidavit for Cause"**. This requires a written statement with reasons and examples given as to why that particular judge is prejudiced against you. A hearing on your affidavit is usually heard by another judge. There is no limit on this type of affidavit. However, they are hard to prove. Sometimes, the judge will grant the affidavit to save time, or will disqualify himself to avoid having a record of such affidavits of prejudice filed against him.

A judge may also disqualify himself from hearing your case. If he does disqualify himself, your case will be sent to another judge. If the judge disqualifies himself, you are still allowed to challenge the next judge.

Motions of various kinds may also be made at the arraignment or before the trial and these are covered in Chapter 18.

The fine is paid after you have been sentenced. If you have posted bail, the fine will be taken out of the bail. Otherwise you will usually be sent or taken, either alone or in a group, to the cashier's office to pay.

The subject of penalties is covered in more detail in Chapter 18—Punishment.

CHAPTER SEVEN

PRETRIAL PREPARATION

The more prepared you are the more comfortable you will feel, the clearer you will think and the more likely you will WIN!.

Pretrial preparation is the most important step in winning in traffic court. It is at this time that you make sure you are ready to make the proper legal motions and are ready for trial. Your pretrial preparation actually should have started when you got the ticket. Your observations of the area, your taking the necessary photographs and obtaining the statements of your witnesses was pretrial preparation.

•Now that you have a trial date go over your statements and the statements of your witnesses. Outline the statements in a step by step manner so that you can question your witness from the statement. Be sure that your witnesses' statements do not convict you. If they cannot help you than do not use them. You are not required to call any witnesses. Also, do not bring them to court with you. If the prosecution finds out that you have witnesses in court she may decide to question them, which is quite proper. They could then be used as prosecution witnesses against you.

•Judges tend to be suspicious of anything that is read. That is one of the main reasons we have not given lists of suggested questions to use in the other chapters. Make sure the outline covers everything, including reference to your photos and diagrams.

•Study the section of the law governing the offense with which you are charged.

Write down each element in a check list that you can follow in a outline form. For example: if you are charged with going over 55 mph the law will probably read, "No person shall drive a vehicle upon a highway at a speed greater than 55 miles per hour (California Vehicle Code 22349)." The elements of the offense are: no person (can you be identified as the driver?); shall drive (were you driving?); a vehicle (were you on horseback?); upon a highway (was your vehicle on a highway?); speed greater than 55 miles per hour (how fast were you going?).

That way you can follow the officer's testimony and check to see if he has covered all the necessary elements of the crime. If he forgets any of these elements then the case may not have been proved and you should be found not guilty. Be careful, in your questioning or testimony not to supply the necessary elements yourself. This happens all too frequently. Do not testify if you are going to convict yourself.

A legal saying is: "Do not ask a question to which you do not already know the answer."

•Diagrams may be used by the officer in her testimony. She may use a blackboard or a magnetic board with toy cars. In some cases, she may use a large sheet of paper to make a diagram and use it to illustrate her testimony. You may do the same thing (see Figure 4). It is preferable to use a diagram on paper in case you decide to appeal. If you intend to use your own diagram be sure it is cleanly and clearly drawn. Use a ruler and dark pen. Be sure that it shows what you want it to show. Prepare it before the trial date.

If you have taken photographs be sure that they are developed. It helps to have them enlarged to at least a 5" x 7" size, if possible.

If the shape of the area or intersection is critical to your case you may be able to obtain an aerial photograph of the area from the city or county department of engineering.

•Try out your statement on someone else. Be sure to tell them ahead of time not to be nice. You need an honest, critical opinion.

Review again your statement, diagram, photos and the law to be sure you don't convict yourself. Many times, it is better to remain silent and not testify. If you do get up on the stand and testify you will be giving up your right to remain silent. If you have prepared properly you may be able to establish your case from using your diagrams and photos along with questioning the officer or your own witnesses.

Practice your statement aloud. I know you may feel silly doing so, but it really helps. You may not be allowed to read from your statement. It is better not to do so. You don't need to parrot what you have written. Use the statement as a guideline so you don't forget your main points.

•If you think you want to cross-examine (question) the officer, then write down the questions you want to ask, in outline form. DO NOT make a statement of what you want to say. Ask a question! For example: do not start by saying, "I was going down the street and stopped at the stop sign". Try instead, "Officer, were you moving or parked? Were there other cars on the road? Where was I in relation to the stop sign when you first saw me?", etc.. Remember, you will get to hear what the officer has to say before you get a chance to question him or testify yourself.

Your questions will probably change once the

officer testifies anyway. Try not to be too surprised if what you hear isn't what you think happened. Different people see things differently and a few lie.

•Remind your witnesses of the court date, the time, and the location. If you can, go together.

If one of your witness needs a subpoena (an order of the court to appear) you must serve him with it prior to the trial. (See Figure 3.) A subpoena is rarely used by the defense (you) in a traffic court trial. It is usually used when one of your witnesses needs it to show to his employer to get off work the day of the trial or you need to have some physical item or document produced to use as evidence. It may be important and if you need to use a subpoena see APPENDIX B—The Subpoena.

•Get to court sober. Skip the "dutch courage." It isn't safe or smart. You would be surprised how sensitive the court personnel are to the conduct of the people in court. Remember, the bailiff's job is to keep order in the court and that means he is continually watching the courtroom. If you are intoxicated, he will make sure the judge knows it. If you are too far gone you may be arrested.

•Check your car, work and baby sitter arrangements the day before your court date. Make sure everything is working and everyone is ready. Pick out your clothes. Review your material once and put it where you will not forget it. You have already prepared for your court appearances by using a practice run and going for your arraignment so you are probably as ready as you can be and you can be assured that you are more prepared than most people who go to court.

There may be a additional court appearance set at the arraignment in addition to the trial date. This appearance is sometimes called a "Pretrial Conference". This hearing is designed, usually for more serious misdemeanors. The purpose of the Pretrial Conference is to give the court the opportunity to settle cases. This is done by having the prosecution talk with the defense to see if some sort of agreement about the case can be reached. This is where any offers to reduce charges, fines, point counts, traffic schools and so on can be negotiated.

This conference may be optional and if all you want is your trial you ask for a trial date when the judge indicates he wants to set the case for Pretrial. That will save you an appearance. In addition, most cases can be negotiated up until you start the trial.

There are some judges who will insist on your either pleading guilty or going through with the trial if you have not settled the case at the Pretrial Conference. This practice doesn't make much sense but it does happen.

RELAX! Remember, this is only a traffic ticket. The court handles so many of these that your case has no special significance to the judge. If you had just paid the ticket you would have already have lost wouldn't you? So cheer up and get ready to WIN.

ATTORNEY OR PARTY WITHOUT ATTORNEY (NAME AND ADDRESS):   TELEPHONE NO.:   FOR COURT USE ONLY

ATTORNEY FOR (NAME):

Insert name of court, judicial district or branch court, if any, and post office and street address.

Title of Case:

SUBPENA (CRIMINAL OR JUVENILE)

☐ DUCES TECUM

CASE NUMBER:

THE PEOPLE OF THE STATE OF CALIFORNIA, TO (NAME):

1. **YOU ARE ORDERED TO APPEAR AS A WITNESS in this action as follows unless you make a special agreement with the person named in item 3:**

   a. Date: Time: ☐ Dept.:   ☐ Div.:   ☐ Room:

   b. Address:

2. and you are
   a. ☐ ordered to appear in person.
   b. ☐ not required to appear in person if you produce the records described in the accompanying affidavit in compliance with Evidence Code sections 1560 and 1561.
   c. ☐ ordered to appear in person and to produce the records described in the accompanying affidavit. The personal attendance of the custodian or other qualified witness and the production of the original records is required by this subpena. The procedure authorized pursuant to subdivision (b) of section 1560, and sections 1561 and 1562, of the Evidence Code will not be deemed sufficient compliance with this subpena.

3. **IF YOU HAVE ANY QUESTIONS ABOUT THE TIME OR DATE FOR YOU TO APPEAR, OR IF YOU WANT TO BE CERTAIN THAT YOUR PRESENCE IS REQUIRED, CONTACT THE FOLLOWING PERSON BEFORE THE DATE ON WHICH YOU ARE TO APPEAR:**

   a. Name: b. Telephone number:

4. **WITNESS FEES:** You may be entitled to witness fees, mileage, or both, in the discretion of the court. Contact the person named in item 3 **AFTER** your appearance.

DISOBEDIENCE OF THIS SUBPENA MAY BE PUNISHED BY A FINE, IMPRISONMENT, OR BOTH. A WARRANT MAY ISSUE FOR YOUR ARREST IF YOU FAIL TO APPEAR.

For Court Use Only

Dated: . . . .   _____
                                        (Signature of person issuing subpena)

                              . . . .
                                        (Type or print name)

                              . . . .
(See reverse for proof of service)   (Title)

Form Adopted by Rule 982   **SUBPENA**
Judicial Council of California
Revised Effective July 1, 1980   **(CRIMINAL OR JUVENILE)**   76S806C- CR44JC (1)(Rev. 7/80) PS 2-84

SUBPOENA

FIGURE 3

CHAPTER EIGHT

COURT TRIAL

To paraphrase a well-known song, "Get to the court on time", at least thirty minutes early to be sure to get parking. Go to the restroom, and locate the courtroom. Do not forget your witnesses, money and materials which you got together during your pretrial preparation.

•Check the court calendar to be sure your name is on it. The calendar is usually located on the wall outside the courtroom. If you do not see your name go to the traffic clerk's office immediately and tell them. A clerk will check and try to straighten things out.

•When the courtroom opens have a seat. It is only necessary to check in with the bailiff if you are late. He is the person in the uniform. His desk is usually in a corner of the courtroom inside the railing (see Figure 2). If the bailiff is not present in the courtroom and you are late you can check in with the courtroom clerk. Do not interrupt the clerk, just go up to her and wait until questioned. Otherwise, just have a seat.

Now that the trial is here you are probably feeling nervous. Even though you have followed the suggestions in the earlier chapters and are more prepared than most people who go to court you are still nervous. This feeling is perfectly natural. In fact, it is common to most lawyers before they start a trial. Relax! It's going to be O.K.. We are going to guide you through a court trial step by step.

•When your name is called answer, "Ready", in a voice loud enough to be heard. The judge is usually checking to see who is there before starting any trials. The police officer will, usually, indicate if he is present. If he doesn't answer the judge may wait about twenty minutes and will call the case again (this is called "second call"). You answer, "ready" again. If the officer is present the judge will eventually call the case for trial. If the officer doesn't answer then the case will usually be dismissed and you have won. The court may hear other cases before finally calling your case. Be patient.

•If you have to leave the courtroom for any reason before or after your name is called be sure to tell the bailiff and tell him when you have returned. If the court takes a recess, which is a break in the proceedings, you may go outside but return when the bailiff announces that court is again in session. It is important to keep checking as such a recess can be longer or shorter than the judge has stated. It is up to you to be present when court starts up again.

A recess is called for many reasons. Just because the judge is not on the bench, it does not mean that the court is not working. Conferences are held between the defense, the prosecution and the judge and the court personnel get a chance to catch up on paperwork as well as to use the restroom.

Negotiations about your case may take place at any time up to a verdict. During the period of a recess or while waiting for "second call" the prosecuting attorney may wish to talk to you about your case. He may perhaps offer to reduce the charge or allow you to go to traffic school, or ask you questions about the case. Remember, he is NOT your friend. His job is to convict you. Unless you are charged with a serious misdemeanor, a reduction in charge won't mean anything. You could have had traffic school earlier. Probably he is trying to convince you to enter a plea to avoid the trial and most likely because the police officer has not shown up. Remember, if you say anything to him about the case he could use it against you in court if you testify differently and, of course, you will have told him your defense so he can question his witness accordingly.

HOWEVER, if your purpose in demanding a trial was to try and deal your case, especially if the officer did show up, now would be the time to do so. You may be able to negotiate a reduction in your "point count" or make an agreement that if you plead guilty, the fine would be reduced or suspended. You will not be able to enter such negotiations after a conviction, although you may try to persuade the judge to treat you similarly.

Continuances are motions to have the case heard on another date. If the officer is not present and a request is made to continue the case object by saying, "I object to a continuance". You will, usually, not be asked to explain why you object. You are entitled to a speedy trial. However, if the case has been set beyond the speedy trial time limits, you may explain; for example, that you have two small children for whom you have made special arrangements for today and it would be a hardship to you to have the case continued (It is unlikely that the prosecutor will ask and that the judge would grant a continuance in a simple traffic case).

•When your name is called go past the railing called the "bar" separating the audience from the courtroom—now you know what it means when they talk about lawyers passing the bar. Have a seat at the end of counsel table as indicated in Figure 2. The defendant always takes the seat furthest from the witness stand and jury box.

The police officer will be called, sworn and will have a seat in the witness stand. He will be asked to state and spell his name (you and your witnesses will be doing the same later or you may have been sworn in with the entire audience who is going to testify).

If there is a possibility of there being more witnesses than the one police officer you should make a **"Motion to Exclude Witnesses"** and **"Admonish Them Not To Discuss the Case"**. You do this by saying, "I move that witnesses be excluded and admonished." This means that any witnesses, including yours, are to be excluded from the courtroom and told not to discuss the case or their testimony. This will prevent them from hearing the testimony and supposedly from, talking about their testimony outside in the hallway.

Remember, that you and your witnesses have probably discussed the case previously. If, when your witnesses testify, they are asked if they have talked to anyone about this case they should be honest and answer correctly that "yes, they have". The question is used to get a witness embarrassed enough to deny such discussion. This, of course, discredits anything that the witness says thereafter—after all he was lying wasn't he?

When a witness is called to the witness stand he cannot say anything until he is questioned. In fact, if the witness starts to testify without a question being asked this is objected to as **"no question pending"**. If the witness tries to give a answer to a question which has not been specifically asked , you say, "I object — **nonresponsive"**.

Generally the only exception to this rule is when the defendant who is representing herself testifies. In this case, the testimony may be given in a narrative form and not in the "question and answer" form. It would obviously be difficult for you to ask yourself questions and then answer them.

Direct Examination is that part of the trial where the witness is questioned by the person calling him as a witness. In other words, the questions the prosecutor asks the police officer after calling him to the stand to testify is "direct examination". If there is no prosecutor, the judge may question the officer. The officer is only a witness and cannot testify or ask questions. If he tries to do so you should object saying, "I object, the officer has no standing to ask questions. He is not a attorney." This objection is rarely used since it will probably irritate the judge. However, it is perfectly proper and may be necessary to prevent the officer from just saying what he wants or from questioning you or your witnesses.

Cross-examination is the part of the trial where the opposing party questions the witness. This occurs after the person asking the questions on direct examination says that he has "no further questions." In your trial, when the prosecution is done questioning the officer you may then question him and the same applies to your witnesses and you.

The most common mistake which really irritates most judges is for the defendant to start making a statement of their case instead of questioning the officer. You would ask, for example, "Could you see the stop sign from where you were parked?" NOT, "You couldn't see me because of the little building, etc." You cannot be told what questions to ask because each case is different. The chapters dealing with the specific violations will give you a good idea of things to look for in planning your questioning. As mentioned before make a list of questions covering every detail that you can think of and reference it to your photographs and diagrams.

Do not get angry, irate or nasty when you are questioning the officer. Doing so will be only get the judge irritated and get you a guilty verdict. Stay calm and when you are done with your cross-examination say, "Thank you, no further questions." Keep it polite, even though you are seething. Wait until you are outside of the courthouse before you scream and curse.

When you have finished your "Cross-examination" the officer may be asked more questions by the prosecutor or the judge. This is called **"Re-Direct"**. When he is done you may ask him some more questions, which is called **"Re-Cross"**. This should end the questioning although it could go on for a while. When the questioning of the officer is over, and the prosecution has no other witnesses the prosecution's case is over and they **"Rest"**.

You must be very careful in asking questions that you do not remind the officer that he has forgotten an essential element of the case and thus convict yourself. "No Questions" is usually the best tactic unless you are looking for something very specific and are careful how you conduct your questioning.

This writer once saw a case where the judge did not understand how the crime had been committed until after detailed cross-examination by the defense. It then became perfectly clear how the crime had been committed and the defendant was found guilty.

Objections to questions are made where a question is asked in an improper manner or testimony is asked for which should not be allowed for various reasons. Objections, other than the hearsay objection, are rarely of use in a court trial because the judge will probably not be affected by the objectionable testimony.

The test is, "will the requested testimony be harmful (prejudicial) to your case?" There is no need to object in any kind of a trial unless it will be of actual help to you. All that happens if you object to everything that is objectionable is that you get the judge or the jury mad at you. However, if you do not object to an objectionable question, you will have given up (waived) your right to complain about the question and its answer later.

Four of the most commonly used objections are:

•Hearsay: That is when the witness is asked to say what some other person, not a witness in court, said to prove a fact in the case. This is probably one of the most important and most confusing of all the objections. For instance, the officer is asked, "What did Mr. Spectator say?" You object, saying, "I object,— hearsay." The reason is Mr. Spectator is not present and cannot be cross-examined. This is particularly important in speeding cases where the officer will try to testify that his radar or speedometer was calibrated by someone else. What he is told is hearsay. (This is greatly oversimplified; it takes lawyers a great deal of time to understand the full concept of this objection and its exceptions, which are many).

•Conclusion or Speculation: This occurs when the witness is asked to make a conclusion or guess when it is up to the judge or jury to draw those conclusions from the testimony that they have heard.

• **Lack of Foundation**: Sometimes, the witness may not give a particular answer without the prosecution having asked certain "foundational" questions which thereafter allow the officer to answer the question. For example, in order to testify as to the results of radar, the officer must have testified as to his training and experience in the use of radar. If these items have not been shown his answer as to the speed from the radar unit is not allowed, if you remember to object and say, "I object—lack of foundation."

• **Leading Questions**: This means that on Direct Examination the person asking the questions is putting the words in the witness's mouth. Instead of asking, "What happened?" the question, "Did you see Mr. Defendant going through the red light?" is leading. You object by saying, "I object,—leading question."

There are other objections but these are the most common. However, if you do not object at the time the objectionable question is asked then you have given up your right to object later.

Remember only object when it is necessary and helpful to your case and do not wait to object until after the answer.

If the question is answered while you are in the process of objecting or before you have a chance to object you make a **"Motion to Strike The Testimony"**. This will legally remove the answer from consideration by the judge or jury.

The officer may be asked to use a blackboard which is commonly found in courtrooms. It may have toy cars and markers which can be used to illustrate the scene. Or he may be asked to use a large piece of paper on which he will prepare a diagram.

If you wish the officer to use your photo or diagram when you question him or have your witnesses use them, you would ask to have the photographs or diagrams marked as exhibits. Prosecution exhibits are marked by number (1, 2, etc.). Defense exhibits are marked by alphabet (A, B, C, D, etc.). They are then referred to by name: that is; "Defendant's A or B", "Prosecution's 1", etc..

The Defense, your turn, occurs after the prosecution has "rested".

A **"Motion for Acquittal"** may be made at the end of the people's case, after they have rested. This means that if you feel that the case against you has not been proved you ask the judge for a finding of not guilty. Simply say, "I move for an acquittal on the grounds that the people have not proved their case beyond a reasonable doubt." If the judge grants the motion you win. If he denies the motion then you may proceed with your case.

It is usually wise to have any witnesses you may wish to have testify do so before you testify. You have to decide if you need to testify and can only do so after all the witnesses have been called. You should try to present the witnesses in a logical order so that it is easy for the judge to follow your case. You conduct the direct examination and the prosecution will cross-examine them when you have finished.

If you wish to have your witnesses refer to your photographs and/or diagrams you should show them to the witness as you did to the police officer and refer to them by name, for example; "Mr. Smith could you show the judge on Exhibit A what you are referring to".

Witnesses, including yourself, should remember to tell the truth. When so doing it is practically impossible to get your stories confused.

Witnesses should be sure that they understand the question. If the witness does not understand the question he should say so. The witness should also just answer the question. There is no need to volunteer information. You know what you wish to ask him and should have discussed it with him previously. There is nothing wrong with doing this in preparation for trial. It is wrong for the witness to be told what to say. In addition, the witness should wait until he is sure that the complete question has been asked before answering. The witness should also pause slightly before answering which will give you a chance to object if you feel that the question was objectionable.

You may call an "expert witness". This is person who can give an opinion as to a specific issue about which he has special training. He is rarely a percipient or eye witness; that is, he was not present at the time of the alleged offense. In order for such a witness to testify he must "qualify" as an expert. You qualify the witness by asking him questions regarding his training, experience and expertise in the particular field in question. You should have talked with him before the trial so you know what questions to ask. Expert witnesses may be called for different purposes, from attacking radar, to equipment violations. However, they are expensive. If you are indigent you might be able to get the court to pay for the expert by making a motion to appoint and pay for an expert. This is unlikely in most traffic cases.

The testimony of an expert witness was responsible, in a 1985 case, for the reversal of the conviction of a man for the equipment violation of having his win-dows tinted. In fact the California Court of Appeals declared that law to be uncon-stitutional. (People v. Fink, (85), 189 CA3d Supp 1)

After you have finished with your testimony you may be cross-examined by the prosecuting attorney or the judge, not the police officer. If there is no prosecuting attorney and the officer starts to question you, object that the police officer is not an attorney and has no right to question you in court. You, on the other hand, in representing yourself (**in propria persona**) are in fact an attorney.

Answer all questions truthfully. If the question may be answered yes or no, do so. Don't volunteer information. If you feel an explanation is called for you may explain after the questioning is done. Do not get angry or let the prosecutor bait you into losing your temper. Simply keep calm and answer honestly. If you are telling the truth it is practically impossible to get you confused. Take a deep breath. This part is scary and nerve wracking. Just remember, they can't hurt you. It is only a traffic ticket.

When the prosecution is finished with cross-examination you may respond to any issues you feel need answering with further testimony. This is called redirect examination. You may then be questioned again by the prosecution. This is called recross-examination.

When you are all done, wipe the sweat away. You will then return to your seat at the counsel table. The judge will ask if there are any more witnesses or if you rest? You answer accordingly. You probably will have been the last witness for the defense, so when you have finished with your testimony and the prosecution is done with cross-examination, say, **"Defense Rests"** and go sit down.

The officer may be recalled to the stand to answer further questions raised by your testimony. This is called **"rebuttal testimony"**. He may be cross- examined by you just as before.

When both sides have rested, the case may be argued. The prosecutor has the right to the opening or first argument stating why she feels that you are guilty. She may choose not to argue. If you give up your right to argue that ends the case and the judge will rule. If you wish to exercise your right to argue you may then state why you are not guilty. Be brief! List your points simply and clearly. The prosecutor may have a closing argument answering your argument. It is then over. You don't have to argue the case if you don't want to. Just say so when the judge asks you.

Congratulations, you have made it though regardless of what verdict the judge makes. If NOT GUILTY, congratulations again. Go home. Relax. You have won and your bail money will be refunded.

If Guilty, the judge will sentence you. If you have already posted bail he will probably apply what has been posted. He may give you a break on the fine because of your having had the trial, if he feels that you have learned from the experience. A GOOD ATTITUDE is critical at this point. Rarely will the judge increase the fine over the amount of the bail. If you have not posted bail you should have the appropriate amount of cash, a good check or a credit card with you. You will go or be taken to the clerk's office to pay the fine. If you don't have enough money you may ask for an extension of time to pay. If you do not have any means of paying a fine be sure to tell the judge and ask if you can work it off be doing some form of community service (see Chapter 16—Punishment).   A refund of all or part of your bail will take about six to eight weeks.   Make sure that the clerk has your correct address before leaving.   Go home and Relax!!

If you lose, you may file an **appeal** from the judge's decision.   This is usually a futile act.   But not necessarily.   If you intend to appeal you should consult an attorney.   (See APPENDIX D—Appeals.)

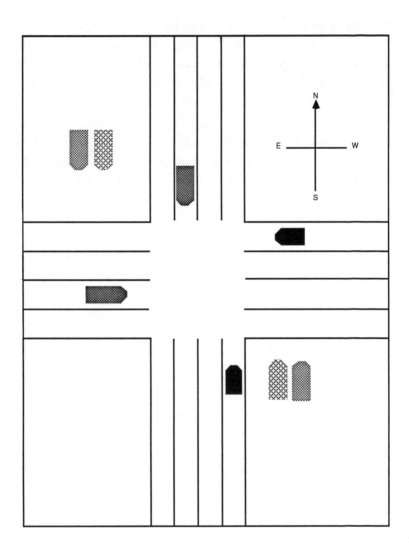

TRAFFIC DIAGRAM

FIGURE 4

CHAPTER 9

JURY TRIALS

A Jury Trial is a trial in which the decision of guilt or innocence is determined by a group of individuals called a jury.

Jury Trials are only available in those traffic cases which are punishable by a jail sentence as well as a fine. Different states have different forms of classification of offenses and call them by different names. For convenience these cases will be referred to as misdemeanors and felonies. *Felony jury trials are exactly the same as misdemeanor jury trials. No examples are given because if you are charged with a felony you should be represented by a lawyer.*

Usually, if the traffic offense is minor and does carry a possible jail sentence, the judge and/or the prosecution will declare at the arraignment that there is no possibility of jail. They do this in order to avoid having to appoint counsel and grant a jury trial.

If you are demanding a jury trial and/or an appointed attorney you may object to this procedure. If the judge overrules (denies) your objection, you can most likely successfully challenge his ruling on appeal since the legislature by so designating the offense as a jailable misdemeanor made a jury trial and appointed counsel available. The major question you should ask yourself is, "do you really want to take this step?" Because if you do you may find yourself in jail if you lose. This would not appear to be a worthwhile risk.

Jury Trials are similar to court (judge) trials as described in Chapter 8—Court Trials. The obvious difference is that the decision of guilt or innocence, except for a Motion for Acquittal made to the judge, at the end of the prosecution's case, is for the jury to decide. A jury consists of six to twelve people chosen at random from a larger group of jurors (usually twenty-five or thirty people). The judge decides the law and instructs the jury on what law to follow. The jury decides the fact of guilt or innocence, which is called the verdict.

A jury trial is more advantageous than a court trial because most state law requires that the entire jury (twelve people in most states) must be unanimous in their decision. If they cannot agree then they are a **"hung jury"** and will be dismissed and the case reset for trial unless dismissed by the prosecution or the judge. The fact is that in most minor cases, if the jury is "hung" the judge will dismiss the case.

The Constitution of the United States guarantees the right to trial by jury in the IVth Amendment. Because jury trials take a lot longer than court trials and are also more expensive, there are always movements to eliminate or change them. Among the proponents of such changes are judges, prosecutors and legislators. These Constitutional Rights of ours are unique. They should be treasured, not given up for the sake of expediency.

The first major difference between the conduct of a court trial and jury trial is that it is necessary to select the jury. This process is called *"voir dire"* (to tell the truth). What happens is that twelve people are selected at random from a larger group of prospective jurors called a "jury panel" who are present in the courtroom. They have all been sworn to answer all questions put to them truthfully and are seated in the jury box. They are then questioned by the judge, yourself or your attorney and the prosecutor. If a juror indicates from the questioning that he is prejudiced he may be excused for **"cause"** and a new juror selected. If the questioner (other than the judge) just doesn't want the juror to sit in judgment he can exercise a **"peremptory challenge"**. There need be no reason given for such challenge. These peremptory challenges are limited in number, depending on the state and the type of case.

The second major difference is, as mentioned above, that a jury composed (supposedly) of your peers must make a unanimous decision of your guilt or innocence. Do not let the prosecution dissuade you from a jury trial, if available, unless it will really be advantageous to you. This is rare. The prosecutor will try to talk you out of your right to a jury trial. You will be told by the prosecutor, using as much legal language as possible, how hard it is to represent yourself and that the trial will take days to be heard (a trial could takes days but the usual traffic type of jury trial with a pro per defendant can and usually is finished in one day.) Neither the prosecutor nor the judge likes it when a defendant represents himself. Do not give up. You can do it.

The third major difference is that a jury trial takes much more time than a court trial. A court trial is usually over in about fifteen minutes whereas a jury trial, as mentioned above, can take all day or longer.

The fourth major difference is that your testimony, objections, statements and argument must be directed to the jury. You must remember that YOU are on trial and must be aware that the jurors are always watching you, even during breaks. Manner, actions, dress, language, etc. are much more important than in a court trial. *The jury must identify with you as much as possible.*

You can see from the above that this is a complicated business, sometimes more of a art form than
anything else. *The services of a lawyer is recommended if you find yourself in such a situation.*

However, if you wish to give it a try, here are
the main procedures and some tips.

Everything, mentioned in Chapter 8—Court
Trial applies only more so.

**Jury selection is also called "voir dire"(to speak
the truth) and will proceed in the following manner:**

•A large number of potential jurors will be
called into the courtroom. They will all be sworn to
answer all questions put to them truthfully, and fully.
Twelve people will be picked at random and seated in
the jury box. You will be given a chart to mark in
their location and names (see Figure 5.).   The judge
will tell the jury the name of the case (People versus
You), the charge and introduce the prosecutor and you
to the jury.

•She may also ask if there are any witnesses to
be introduced. You do not and should not introduce
your witnesses. You do not know if and when you
will be using them. If you introduce a witness and
then do not call him the jury will wonder why and
this could damage your case.

•The judge will then ask a series of questions of
the jurors. She will probably ask each juror to give his
name, the city he lives in, his occupation and that of
his spouse, and if he has had any prior jury experience. She will then ask them generally if they will
follow the law and if they understand the *presumption of innocence until proven guilty beyond a reasonable doubt.* She may ask more questions; this varies considerably. When the judge is finished, she will
ask you if you have any questions of the jury.

•While some questions can be asked of the entire jury, each juror should have some questions asked of him individually. It is necessary to do this to establish a rapport with the juror and get a feel for what he is saying.

•The questions asked by you are to determine if you wish that person to be the judge of the facts in your case; to determine if they are prejudiced against you.

•You always want to ask if they have had any legal training; if they have friends or family in law enforcement; if they are drivers; if they have been involved in any traffic accidents and feel that this may have an effect on their hearing the case; if they feel that because you are charged with a crime, that you are guilty; that is, do they understand that you are presumed innocent until proven guilty beyond a reasonable doubt; will they agree that they have a duty to wait until they hear all the evidence, the arguments, and the law before they start to reach any conclusions other than that you are presumed innocent. If you are a member of a minority or feel that there is something unusual about your appearance, do not be afraid to ask if this will affect the juror.

Frankly, this writer feels that this is the hardest and probably the most important part of a jury trial. The main thing is that you are trying to get a feel for the jurors. It is rare when a juror will admit that he or she is prejudiced. If they indicate that they may be so prejudiced and that they do not wish to hear the case, the judge will ask, "will you follow the law?" They almost always answer, "yes". Then he asks, "do you feel that you can put your feelings aside and be a fair and impartial juror?" They usually answer, "yes". Then the judge will refuse to excuse that juror for cause; that is, because he cannot be fair. You then have to use your peremptory challenge as mentioned earlier. If you get a feeling that the juror should not hear your case ask that he be **excused** ("kick him off the jury"). You would say "I thank and excuse Mr. Doe, juror number X." When you and the prosecutor are satisfied with the jury, you will say that you **"accept the jury"**.

If you have used up your peremptory challenges you will have no choice as to when to accept the jury. Always ask before the jury comes into the court room how many challenges you are allowed. It varies depending on penalty and state. Six peremptory challenges are common if less than a ninety day jail sentence and ten if more.

After the twelve jurors have been selected the judge may have one to two alternate jurors selected. They are questioned similarly to the other jurors. They will not take part in the deliberations of the jury unless some member of the jury has to be excused for some valid reason.

Once the jury has been selected, the procedures of trial are just about the same as listed in Chapter 8— Court Trial. *The major difference is that you, the prosecutor, and the witnesses will be addressing your statements to the jury, except for objections.* An objection calls for the judge to make a ruling of law. It is the judge who decides whether the question or answer was objectionable. Sometimes an obviously objectionable question will be asked even when it is known that the judge will order the jury to disregard it. The feeling is that you have made your point anyway. This is not proper conduct. This is especially important to remember when you are on the witness stand and when you are arguing the case.

Talk to the jury when your witnesses or you are

testifying, not the prosecutor or the judge. If the prosecutor is getting you mad on cross-examination, keep calm. If you get mad and show it you may lose whatever sympathy the jury will feel over the prosecution trying to browbeat you.

•**Jury instructions are statements of the law which is applicable to your case.** The jury should follow these instructions in reaching a verdict. (See Figure 6). Before the final argument, the judge will ask you and the prosecutor if you wish any special jury instructions other than the standard set of instructions.

There is usually a standard set of instructions from which the judge will read. These instructions will include general statements of law including the presumption of innocence and reasonable doubt. There will also be a statement which gives the law regarding the specific crime with which you have been charged. If you, or the prosecutor, have any instructions which are different from the standard instructions, now is the time to show them to the judge to see if he will use them. In most cases, the standard instructions are sufficient. If your case is sufficiently complicated to need special instructions, you really need a lawyer.

•**Final argument is just like that in a court trial.** There is an opening argument by the prosecutor, your argument and the closing argument by the prosecutor.

When arguing to the jury, remember to emphasize how the burden of proof is on the prosecution, that you are innocent unless and until each element of the case has been proven against you beyond a reasonable doubt and that you do not have to prove anything beyond a reasonable doubt. You will then state why these elements have not been proven.

Keep your argument brief and hit all the points

that you have been keeping track of during the trial. Do not forget to show the jury your photographs explaining what they show. Also, remember to use your diagrams. In a jury trial it is usually a good idea to have the diagrams on paper so that the jury can take them into the jury room so that they can be used during deliberations.

In addition, you should mention to the jury that this will be the only chance that you will have to argue the case. Therefore, if they feel that you have left a question unanswered, ask them to consider the evidence and try to answer it in your favor.

•Since you are representing yourself always remember that the jury will be observing you at all times, including during recesses (DO NOT talk to them or let your witnesses talk to them!). Try to present yourself in as favorable a manner a possible. Dress conservatively, get a hair cut, avoid emotional outbursts and follow the rules as set forth above.

When the jury has given its verdict you may talk with the jurors if you wish, if they are still around and wish to talk with you. It can be very interesting to find out how and why they reached their verdict.

If you have been found guilty of the charge, the judge will sentence you. (See Chapter 16—Punishment.) You do have a right to appeal from the verdict and sentence. (See APPENDIX D—APPEALS.)

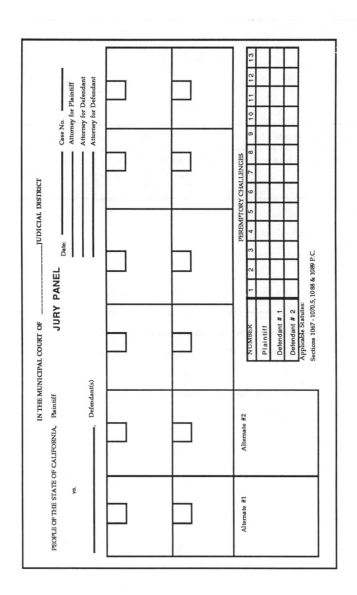

JURY SELECTION SHEET

FIGURE 5

CALJIC 4.50

ALIBI

Requested by People		Given as Requested		Refused	
Requested by Defendant		Given as Modified		Withdrawn	
		Given on Court's Motion			

Judge

4.50

The defendant in this case has introduced evidence tending to show that he was not present at the time and place of the commission of the alleged offenses for which he is here on trial. If after a consideration of all the evidence, you have a reasonable doubt that the defendant was present at the time the crime was committed, he is entitled to an acquital.

JURY INSTRUCTIONS

FIGURE 6

CHAPTER 10

SPEEDING AND GOING TOO SLOW

Speeding is the most common of the moving violations. *There are two types of speeding laws: Maximum (minimum) Laws specify the maximum and/or minimum speeds at which a vehicle may be operated. The Basic Speed Laws (Prima Facie) are designated as being "safe" speeds for the posted area.*

Maximum (minimum) violations occur when the driver goes either above or below the designated speed. There is no defense, except for possibly an emergency situation. For example, as this book was being written, 55 mph was the maximum speed limit in most states. The Wisconsin Motorists Handbook, for example, states "Wisconsin speed limits are absolute—they must not be exceeded." Federal Park speed limits are also absolute. Common speeds that are set are: 15 mph in a school zone when children are present; 25 mph in a residential area; 35 mph in a business zone. Each state varies and you should check to be sure.

States which permit a faster speed will lose federal highway funds. The 1987 Congress did finally pass, overriding a presidential veto, a highway bill which permits the states to make certain exceptions to this speed and raise the speed limit to 65 mph in non-urban areas. It is no defense to say to the judge that you were going with the *"flow of traffic"* which just happened to be going faster that 55 mph. We all know that this law is probably the most frequently violated in the country anywhere and anytime.

Most basic speed laws require that "you must drive at a speed that is reasonable and prudent". Think about other traffic, surface and width of the road, dangers at intersections, weather, visibility and any other existing conditions. You can violate the basic rule even though you are not going faster than a designated speed or posted speed if "a lower speed is needed to make up for heavy traffic, poor visibility, slippery roads or some other hazardous condition." (Oregon Driver's Manual 1984-85 ed.) With these types of speed limits you can be going faster than the designated speed (not posted but specified for that area such as mentioned above for schools, residential areas, etc.) or posted speed if you can show that the conditions were safe to do so. That is why it was recommended earlier that as soon as you get a ticket for speeding you immediately note the conditions of the area and take note of the speed of the other traffic. Here "going with the flow" may help.

The officer will always write on the ticket the basic (or maximum/minimum) speed for the area and what speed he feels that you were going. He will make a note of the traffic and road conditions, for example; medium traffic and light rain. He will also note what speed he feels would be safe for that area and time. If you feel that he is not correct as to your speed because it disagrees with what you observed on your speedometer you should consider calibrating your speedometer.

At the trial the officer will probably testify that his speedometer was calibrated fairly recently. *Trial note: if the officer was not present when the calibration was done you may object to his testimony as "hearsay".* It should not be admitted into evidence since he, personally, doesn't know it was done and he was told by someone who is not a witness what the calibration was. The evidence may be introduced by showing the appropriate business records but the officer rarely has them available.

Many automobile clubs have a calibration service available at no or low cost to their members. Otherwise, you should have the calibration done, in your presence, at a speciality shop (where it may also be readjusted if necessary). You may also calibrate it yourself by measuring your time at a certain speed over a measured distance. Most states have such areas on the highways. Remember that accurate calibration for one speed does not mean that the speedometer is accurate at all other speeds. Also, your odometer (distance meter) is also probably not very accurate for exact distance. Still it is better than nothing. Both the speedometer and odometer are dependent on the size of your tires. If you are using nonstandard tires then the speedometer reading can be quite inaccurate.

> *This writer remembers being stopped for speeding in Missouri. The speedometer had indicated 55mph but the officer said he had both paced and clocked the vehicle at 60. He said that the tires looked oversize which they were and gave me a warning. He also assisted in calibrating my speedometer with his radar. The result—55 was actually 60 mph.*

If you lose the trial or decide to plead guilty with an explanation and can show that your speedometer was off and that you have had it corrected, this will probably influence the judge into a lower or even suspended fine. You are, however, responsible for the condition of your vehicle.

Speed violations are determined by the police officer making a judgment call as to what he considered a safe speed for that area and a determination of whether you are going faster than that speed. Obviously the maximum speed is already set but even then a lot of discretion is used by the officers. Unfortunately motorcycles, sports cars and expensive luxury cars all stand out from the crowd and will be susceptible to more tickets.

Three ways are used to determine speed: time through a measured distance, pacing, and radar.

•**Time through a measured distance in a particular area of highway**. This is commonly called a "speed trap" and is not allowed in many states. In a speed trap, the officer sets up in one of four ways. First, he measures a specified distance and then times your passage over that distance with a stop watch. Second, he sets up two rubber air hoses across the street a certain distance apart. Your car will fire one then the other and that will be used to determine speed (these air hoses are mostly used today for traffic surveys). The third method is, "VASCAR" (visual average speed computer and recorder). In this method a timer is connected to a simple distance computer. Once the officer has driven over a specified distance he then operates controls of the machine when you enter and leave the area and the computer will give a speed reading. This is based on his visual perceptions and is not a "radar" system. Since the development of cheap radar units these methods are rarely used anymore. Fourth, Radar used in an area where there has not been a traffic survey has also been held to be a speed trap.

•**Pacing is a method where an officer will try to match the speed of your vehicle with his vehicle and**

then stay with you for as long as he feels necessary. The longer the pace the more accurate it will be. He will note the speed on his speedometer and then stop you. He is not required to pace you for any specified distance.

It is important in these cases to determine how the officer made the pace. For example, if he is speeding up to catch you such as coming from his hiding place on a freeway on-ramp he may be making his determination based on his increasing speed which is not a truly paced speed. If you have noticed the officer coming up behind you and monitored your speedometer, and have not slowed down you may then be able to show that the officer was in error because he was speeding up and you were maintaining a constant legal speed. Don't hit your brakes, your brake light will indicate to the officer that you are slowing.

A good driving tip is to be constantly scanning the front, left and right mirrors and sides, rearview mirror and instruments about every twenty seconds. That way you will know what is going on and can so testify. You will also be able to see the officer in time to note what his actions are. Remember, police love to sit up on on-ramps to freeways, side streets, and bridges. When you zip by, he will accelerate to pull behind and pace you. You can ask if he was stopped when he first observed you and if so, was his ignition on and did he report in on his radio. All these things take time and will distract him from a accurate pace if he can even obtain one. In other words, he may have been reading his accelerating speedometer instead of obtaining a constant pace.

Beware of the **"wolf pack"**. In this situation there are two or more patrol cars. One will pass you or pull a car over to the side of the road. You now feel safe and accelerate. Meanwhile, his partner is coming up behind you. A driver usually gets nailed when he become inattentive or in too much of a hurry.

Aircraft are being used to patrol certain stretches of road. The pilot or observer will time your vehicle over a measured distance, usually a series of markers on the highway, and then call down to a patrol car with the description of the car and the speed. The patrol car will then try to locate that vehicle and make a stop. He will probably also pace you if you are still moving at a high rate of speed. This avoids being a speed trap because it is considered to use all the highway and not one specified section of it.

There are many inherent errors in such observations. The air observer may not be low enough to get a license number and may give the ground officer a physical description of the car which is similar to others depending on traffic. It would be unusual if the air officer could see who was driving the car. It is essential that it be proved that you were driving the car at the speed in question. This is obviously an issue when there are other people in the car. Therefore, at trial be careful not to agree to any statements by the ground officer as to what he was told by the air officer. This is objected to as "hearsay" and is not admissible. Do not take the stand to admit that, "Yes, you were the driver." Both officers must be present to get the air-determined speed and your identity into evidence. Of course, if the ground officer made an independent pace of your speed that is a different matter.

•**Radar is a means of measuring speed electronically.** Because of the wide spread use of these machines the subject will be covered in Chapter 11—RADAR.

There are two types of radios which may be

used to determine whether or not the "coast is clear" or if you are the subject of police attention.

• **"CB" or citizen band radios are used a lot by motorists to give warning of the location of the police and radar units.** Be aware that the police are also using such radios not only to monitor the use of the radios but, in some instances, to trap motorists by giving out statements which would lead one to believe it is safe to speed. Take care. The safest route is still the legal one.

• **"Monitors" are radios which are used to monitor or listen to police radio frequencies.** These frequencies are allocated by the Federal Communications Commission (2025 M Street NW, Washington D.C. 20001) and may be obtained from that organization under the Freedom of Information Act (5 United States Code 552). You can hear if you are the target, if you are on the right frequency and understand what is being said. However, be warned, these units are illegal in many states and you could be facing other criminal penalties in addition to your speeding violation. Check your own state laws and stay legal.

Speeding may be an element within other more serious moving violations; such as Exhibition of Speed, Speed Contests, Reckless Driving, and Driving Under the Influence. These sections are covered under Chapter 14—Other Crimes. For example, an officer may only cite you for speeding if you are going 80 mph on a freeway. He may take you to jail for doing the same on surface streets as this speed could be considered "Reckless Driving" in such an area.

Hiding is part of the game. Beware the sign or side street, trash bin, garbage truck or farm vehicle parked at the side of the road. Officers have been hiding behind or inside such objects and when you zip by radio to their partner to make the stop. The same suggestions apply here as in aircraft stops mentioned previously.

GOING TOO SLOW

Going Too Slow is obviously the reverse of speeding. You may be cited for going too slow if you are going slower than the "flow of traffic" and such is creating traffic hazard; if you are driving in a lane other than one designated for slower traffic (the lane nearest the right shoulder of the roadway is usually set aside for slower traffic); or if you are driving slower than a designated minimum speed. Citations of this type are not too common.

The defense against a charge of driving too slow is similar that of a speeding defense except in reverse. For example:

•You want to show that your speed was safe for the conditions and that the "flow of traffic" was too fast.

•Your speed was necessary for the safe operation of your car due to the type of cargo you were carrying such as delicate equipment, dangerous chemicals, or explosives (be sure you have the necessary permits to carry such items if required).

•Your speed was due to an emergency condition of your car such as a blown tire or engine overheating and that you were moving the vehicle to a position of safety.

•If the roadway is in a dangerous condition such as being wet, or icy or badly rutted or potholed, then a slow speed may be required.

•You had moved into the fast lane only for the

distance necessary to make a left turn.

•If you were driving too slow because you were looking for an address or just sightseeing you are probably out of luck if you were also obstructing traffic.

Certain types of farm equipment are permitted to drive on the highways at very slow speeds. These speeds would apply to ordinary traffic only if you get stuck behind the equipment. Be careful, the frustration of being stuck behind such farm equipment often leads to dangerous driving such as trying to pass where it is not safe. It has been this writer's experience that most drivers of such equipment will pull over and give you a chance to pass as soon as they can.

STOPPING DISTANCES
ON DRY CONCRETE

SPEED Miles per Hour	REACTION TIME BEFORE YOU APPLY BRAKES* Feet	BRAKING DISTANCE Feet		STOPPING DISTANCE Feet
20	22 +	22	=	44
30	33 +	50	=	83
40	44 +	88	=	132
50	55 +	138	=	193
60	66 +	198	=	264
70	77 +	270	=	347

*Assumes zero perception time and a reaction time of 3/4 second. This is optimistic

STOPPING DISTANCES
ON WET FLUSHED ASPHALT
ARE MORE THAN
<u>DOUBLE</u> THE ABOVE

A Football Field is only 300 feet long and the average city block is even shorter. Even at 40 mph it can take you a wholecity block to stop on wet asphalt.

STOPPING DISTANCES
ON ICE AT 25°F.

SPEED Miles per Hour	REACTION TIME BEFORE YOU APPLY BRAKES* Feet	BRAKING DISTANCE Feet		STOPPING DISTANCE Feet
20	22 +	149	=	171
30	33 +	340	=	373
40	44 +	598	=	642
50	55 +	940	=	995

STOPPING DISTANCE CHART

FIGURE 7

CHAPTER 11

RADAR

Radar is a means of measuring speed by bouncing electric signals off of your car and measuring how fast they return. Radar can only measure the difference between the outgoing and the incoming signals. Therefore, the radar unit cannot tell whether the target is approaching or retreating, only the speed with which it is going. This is done automatically by the radar unit.

Radar may be used either stationary or mobile. States like California only allow radar to be used from a stationary position. Other states, like Missouri or Utah, allow radar to be used stationary, from a moving vehicle or hand-held. The stationary units may be attached to the outside of the police car. You may look for a horn shaped object on the rear driver's side or in the rear window pointing, with the wide end, in your direction. The unit may also be mounted on the front dashboard. If you see it it is usually too late. The radar unit may be hand-held. This type is coming into more frequent use especially by motorcycle officers. If you see a motorcycle cop parked at the side of the roadway with a box in his hand it is probably not his lunchbox.

Radar can be imagined as a flashlight beam. The closer to the lens, the narrower the beam and the further away, the wider the beam. Depending on the unit a typical radar beam will have spread out to cover about two lanes of traffic at a distance of about 160 feet (one foot in width for every four feet in distance). The beam width in feet = 17 x maximum range in thousands of feet x beam width in degrees. (This figure will be specified for each machine.)

The radar unit will also read large objects further away from the unit and nonmetallic and smaller objects closer to the unit, such as cars with fiberglass bodies and motorcycles. The radar unit will pick up trees waving in the wind and be affected by rain and thunderstorms. If you are in the area where the beam covers two lanes and there is a car next to you it is not really possible for the officer to tell which vehicle is going faster. If there is a larger faster vehicle such as a truck behind you the radar may pick up that vehicle. but because you are in front the officer interprets the reading as that of your vehicle. Be aware of the possibility of low flying aircraft or trains moving near you for the same reason. If you find yourself being stopped try to observe if any of the foregoing situations apply to you. Then when you go to trial you will be able to establish a doubt that the radar reading was accurate.

A favorite location for a patrol car with a radar unit is just the other side of a bend in the road. *If you spot a radar unit in front of you and you are going fast, slow down, you may indeed be covered by other traffic.* The further away you are, the wider the beam and the more likely other traffic beside you is being measured. If there is a unit behind you and you see it, remember, stepping on your brake turns on your rear brake lights thus signaling to a moving radar unit behind you that you were indeed slowing. Be discrete.

If you see someone pulled over getting a ticket do not think you are automatically safe. The officer can reset the machine to a specific speed with a audible alarm. If it goes off while he is giving a ticket and he see you, you may be next. This "auto-lock" feature is also a source of error in that, if there is more than one vehicle in the area, the officer has no way of knowing which vehicle has triggered the alarm. The officers may also work in groups. They place the radar unit around a curve, or on a bridge or overpass and then radio to other units to pick you up. It does not hurt, when pulled over to ask to see the reading of your speed. If refused, you can bring this up in court. You would treat this situation the same as a "aircraft stop" covered in Chapter 10—Speeding. So be prepared.

The radar unit must be calibrated before use. This is usually done with special "certified" tuning forks which are set for a specific speed. If such calibration is not done then the reading will not be accurate. If the tuning forks have been damaged they will be inaccurate and therefore the calibration of the radar unit will be in error. A question to ask is if they have ever been dropped or scratched. Also some machines have a test in which the machine has a internal check called "calibration" in which a signal is generated internally. This is not a substitute for the use of the set of tuning forks. On cross-examination you should ask if the officer used the machine or the tuning forks to actually calibrate the radar. The calibration should, ideally, be done before and after each citation.

In addition, in order for the testimony of a radar estimate of speed to be admissible a traffic survey must have been fairly recently prepared. This is an item which deals with the area in which you were stopped and determines an average speed for the traffic of the area. If a certified copy of such a traffic survey is not introduced into evidence you should object to the officer's testimony as lacking the proper foundation. However, if the judge has read the traffic survey previously he may be able to take "judicial notice" of its existence. This means that it is not required to be introduced into evidence for the officer to testify. He can still testify as to your speed if he was able to observe it by means of one of the other means of speed estimation such as pacing or timing.

You can see how important it is start your observations of the area as soon as you realize that those police lights are intended for you. When the officer gives you the ticket he will probably tell you that he established your speed by radar. Do not make any statements that can be used against you by the officer, such as "I couldn't have been going that fast, I was going X mph" where X would be too fast any way. Just answer with a "Oh, was that what your radar showed?" You can then carefully question the officer as to where he was when he got the reading, how long he had been at that position and when the machine was calibrated. If he offers to show you the reading be sure to go look. It wouldn't hurt to ask to see the unit and what the reading shows. This will give you a chance to see the type of radar unit, its name, make and possibly its serial number. If it appears that you are provoking the officer, then STOP. Don't insist on his answering your questions. Just make a mental note of what was asked and/or refused so that you can use those observations later when cross-examining the officer.

It is also important to go back to the location. Do this as soon as possible afterwards, preferably about the same time of day, so that you can make sketches, notes and take photographs of your observations. In this way you can prove that the obstacles you are going to ask the officer about are actually there. Then when you question the officer on cross-examination you will be able to establish his location, where he says he first observed you, how much and what type of traffic, weather conditions—rain, thunder, lighting and/or wind, large trees or foliage in the vicinity—low flying aircraft, tv, or radio transmitters, hospitals, power lines, etc.. You can then try to show that he was set up to cover too wide a width of street for catching just your car and that, if there was other traffic, it could be their speed that was measured, or rain, or a waving tree or that there were other sources of interference. In addition, if the officer denies the existence of such obstacles, you can show their existence by your evidence. If the officer is wrong on such items you can argue that he is wrong about your speed.

You cannot really argue that the radar reading of your speed was off because of the angle of the beam; that is, that he was set up so the radar unit was pointed at an angle toward your car, because this means that the reading was actually lower than your actual speed. So stay away from such questions.

Another way an officer can get a speed reading higher than actual when using a hand-held unit, is by raising the unit suddenly to catch you. If he doesn't wait one or two seconds after the unit is raised and steady to get a reading, it will probably be too high because the unit is adding the speed of the arm raising to the speed of the car. Some hand-held units are equipped with pistol grips and sights which give a mistaken impression that the radar unit can be aimed. This can result in an error of observation because the officer may think he is aiming at one car but is actually obtaining a reading from another.

The officer must make an independent observation of oncoming traffic to identify the so-called speeder. Because of the spreading width of the beam the further away the targets are located the less precise will be any identification of the reading with a group of vehicles. The reading will be fairly accurate if there is only one vehicle in the beam at the time and no other interference.

Another error called "shadowing", may occur when the mobile radar unit locks on to other traffic in reading the speed of the patrol car itself. The mobile unit measures two things: your car's speed and the patrol car's motion relative to the ground. It does this by the use of two beams. The high beam is used to measure the signal from the target vehicle and the low beam is used to measure the ground, parked cars or the landscape and is supposed to represent the speed of the patrol vehicle itself. These signals are then compared and a reading is obtained of the target vehicle. If the low beam mistakes a nearby car, truck or trailer for the ground it will add mph to the target speed thus resulting in error.

> *A friend of this writer told of being in a parked patrol vehicle when the officer was demonstrating the radar to him. When the officer put the "gun" on a moving car the readout of the speed of the police car, which was stationary, showed 25 mph. It should have been zero. Therefore, any reading he obtained would be in error.*

"Bumping" is another error which can occur when a patrol car with a mobil unit slows suddenly and turns in order to make a u-turn to go after a target vehicle. The sudden slowing of the vehicle can cause a dipping of the front of the patrol vehicle and thus bump upwards the speed of the target .

Instant On Radar Units can cause a problem in that the officer does not obtain a "traffic history". This traffic history means that by having the radar on prior to attempting to obtain a reading the officer is able to determine if there are any spurious signals such as caused by CB, police radio or sources of electromagnetic interference (EMI) such as from nearby radar, tv or radio transmitters, thunder and lighting storms, high tension wires, power stations or relays or other electrical interference.

Since there are no real standards for beam width of the radar it impossible to determine how wide a range of targets the unit might be covering at the time of the reading unless the officer is making a personal observation and there is really only one car in the beam.

"Harmonic error" can occur in the newer phase-lock loop radar. That is, the unit can double or triple the speed reading of a vehicle moving at 20 miles per hour or less.

In preparing for trial, in addition, to providing diagrams, photos and statement of witnesses you can also obtain, by the use of a *subpoena duces tecum,* many items of useful information. (See Figures 3 and 12 as well as APPENDIX B—The Subpoena). These would be: the radar unit, the tuning fork, the repair, log and calibration records of the radar unit, the officer's training records and certificate to operate the machine, the instruction and specification manuals for the machine as well as any certification for the speedometer of the patrol car.

These items should be requested for a specific date prior to the trial so that you can inspect them and be prepared to use them at the trial. Note that the prosecutor will probably try to argue against the production of these items prior to or at the trial.

If you are hoping that the officer will not appear on the day of trial and that you will be able to get a dismissal then do not plan on using the above the steps in getting the records and machines because the prosecutor as well as the officer will make sure that the officer is present, if at all possible. Anytime that you give the officer reason to believe that you are going to fight the case, he will probably make it a point to be present.

At the trial you can then cross-examine the officer from the information gained from inspection of the various records, especially, to see if he has had the usually required 24 hours of classroom and 16 hours of in field training . If his training records are produced and these requirements are met then don't try to question him on that area as it will only strengthen his testimony.

After you have made whatever points you were trying to make by cross-examination of the officer you will proceed with your defense as you would in any other case with the exception of trying to produce evidence of outside interference as mentioned above.

Remember, even if he is either correct or believed as to your speed you can still defend the case on the theory that your speed was nevertheless safe and reasonable even if faster than the posted basic speed. Except, of course, if you were going faster than a specified maximum speed limit.

The radar unit itself is a radio transmission device and must be licensed by the Federal Communications Commission. If not so licensed it is probably being used illegally. If the officer does not testify to the license and prove its validity by showing a valid license, you should object as to any testimony about the radar unit for "lack of foundation."

You have probably heard about the "Stealth Bomber" which is impervious to radar. You may have wondered if there was something that you could do to your car to get the same effect. There is no practical way to do so. Aluminum foil in the hubcaps, special paint, or dropping metal "chaff" won't work. It is true that radar picks up metal objects and large objects further away than smaller objects such as motorcycles and fiberglass body cars. But it will pick them up and will not be confused by such other items. The only device that is effective is the radar detector.

•**Radar detectors are electronic devices which will pick up a radar signal and warn you of its presence.** They can be effective particularly against stationary radar. They are not much use against moving radar or hand-held radar if the radar units are being used selectively to get a reading on a particular car. However, if they are left on and not used on/off then these units can provide some form of early warning. The advertisements will indicate that the units will pick up both "X" and "K" bands. These refer to the frequencies in which the radar units operate. You should know that at least two states have made the use of such units illegal. They are Connecticut and Virginia. Be sure to check your own state laws.

•**Radar jammers are being advertised**. They will, the ads say, prevent a radar unit from being able to operate effectively. They do this by putting out a strong signal on the same frequency being used by the radar unit. This is illegal. The Federal Communications Commission prohibits such interference. A violation can result in confiscation of the equipment, which could include your car, a fine and/or jail.

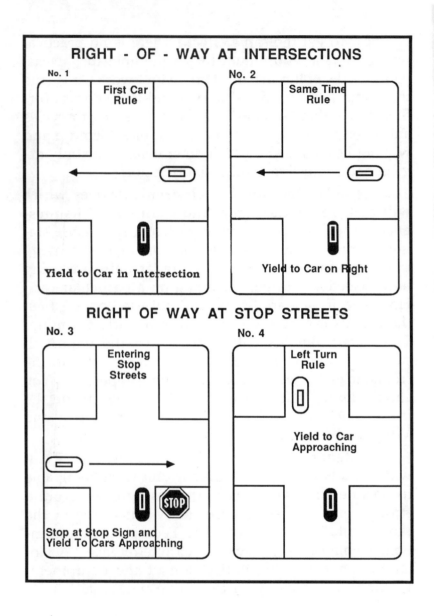

RIGHT OF WAY DIAGRAM

FIGURE 8

CHAPTER 12

RULES OF THE ROAD

Do you know when to pass, in what lane to drive when passing, when and where to stop and go and when to signal and how? These and other driving techniques and laws are known as the "Rules of the Road". They are, with few exceptions, common to all the states. You had to learn them in order to pass your driving test. If you do not follow these rules when driving you are a ticket looking to be written. If you are written up for a violation of these laws you must be familiar with them to know if you have indeed violated them or if the officer was mistaken. With such knowledge you can win in traffic court.

One very important element that is common to all violations of the rules of the road, as well as all other moving violations, is that you must be the individual driving. If the officer cannot or forgets to establish that fact, quit, do not testify and establish it for him. You can rest your case and win. The officer will usually be asked if the person who was driving the car is present in the courtroom and if so to point him out. If he does not identify the defendant—you, as the driver, you win. This is sometimes a good reason for continuing a case.

Stopping or the failure to do so is probably, next to speeding the most common traffic violation.

•The law is clear regarding a stop at a stop sign. *You must come to a complete stop (no forward motion) at or slightly in front of the sign.* Some intersections have "limit lines" which show where to stop. If you find that you are stopped in the intersection you have gone too far and may be cited. You must not proceed until it is safe to proceed. This does not mean that there is no traffic in the cross traffic lanes, only that after you have made a complete stop you must be able to safely accelerate and cross the intersection before causing cross traffic to take steps to avoid you.

The police officer will be looking to see if you have in fact stopped, or if your vehicle is slowed but still in motion (the famous "California Rolling Stop"). If you keep going, you get ticketed. If you stop the other side of the stop sign, you get ticketed. What happens if you did in fact stop properly and get a ticket? This is where it is very important to try to find out where the officer was when he saw you. Check the area for obstructions to his view. Take photos as mentioned before. Then, in court, if he has shown all the elements of a violation of the law, you first try to establish by cross-examination that he couldn't actually see what he thought he saw. Then if that doesn't work present your defense to establish that fact. For example, you stopped early and he couldn't see because of bushes.

In regards to failing to stop or crossing too soon after a complete stop the officer will probably have had his attention drawn to you by the screeching of brakes and the blowing of horns. If he sees other cars suddenly putting on their brakes and the front of the cars dipping sharply then he is safe in assuming that you crossed too early or did not stop. However, if you can establish some other reason for the action of these other vehicles such as as an obstruction in the road, a child darting out, etc. you may have a winning case.

•School buses also have stopping controls which you must follow. If a school bus is displaying flashing lights both oncoming and following traffic must stop in front of or behind the bus and not creep up on it or proceed until the lights are turned off. This does not apply to turn signals. Of course, if you can show that the bus was empty and the driver forgot to turn off the signals and you only proceeded after a full stop and appropriate waiting period, you have a shot at winning. Here it is important to interview the bus driver and subpoena her into court if she is helpful. You can usually locate the name of the driver via the dispatch office by giving the location and time of the incident. Other witnesses to confirm your actions would be most helpful since it would be unusual for a bus driver to admit such conduct to you.

• **Emergency vehicles have the right of way and you must pull over and stop when you see one approaching with the emergency lights and/or siren on**. You are responsible for hearing and seeing it. If you testify that you did not hear the siren because your radio was too loud, you lose. However, if you can show that the vehicle did not in fact have the appropriate signals on when you were stopped you can win. Here it is crucial that you check with people in the area right after getting your ticket to see if they saw the incident and can verify that the emergency vehicle did not in fact have its emergency equipment in operation.

• **Railroad crossing stop signals, either crossing guard gates or flashing red lights require a complete stop.** Failure to do so results in a very high number of deaths every year. You can't beat a train. They move faster than you can imagine.

> *This writer can remember when he was a teenager trying to catch up to and pace a train on a straightaway At 85 mph we quit. The train was still pulling away.*

There are situations where the warning signs

are malfunctioning or have been set off by other than railroad personnel. In these cases it is still wiser to try to use a different crossing if possible as you do not really know that it is in fact safe to cross.

If you have been waiting a long time and do cross, you must be prepared to testify how long you waited for a train to appear and that you only crossed after having checked both directions to be sure it was clear. You can also check with the operator of the railroad company that owns that section to see if any repairs were made during the period when you got that ticket. If so, then you can have those records brought into court by use of a *subpoena dueces tecum* (see APPENDIX B—Subpoenas). You should never try to maneuver around crossing gates. It is too easy to get trapped as well as being illegal.

•**Running a traffic light is probably the most frequent traffic violation after speeding and failing to stop for a stop sign.**

We all know that the red light means stop and the green means go. *It is the middle light, the yellow or amber as it is called, which causes problems.* If the green light turns yellow as you approach the intersection you are supposed to start slowing and eventually stop as the red light comes on. The big "if" here is "if you can safely do so" otherwise you may proceed. If the light is still yellow as you leave the intersection you win as you have not gone through a red signal.

In some states, like California, if you have crossed a limit line, crosswalk, or actually entered the intersection on the yellow before the light has turned red you have not committed a violation. Some states are just the opposite, however, and make it a violation if you are just within the intersection if the red light comes on. The reasoning is that a "yellow light" means to prepare to stop and to start slowing. If you entered the intersection under those conditions you were not in fact slowing and therefore ignoring the caution light and violating the law.

You must check the individual state law. *The best and safest driving practice is to start slowing on a yellow in order to stop at the change and do not run it.* You never know if someone is trying to beat the light from the other direction

Usually, the officer will state that the light had gone to red before you left the intersection. If he was either in front of or behind you he will say that he could actually see the light change before you left the intersection. You have to show that from where he was located his perception of where you were was in error. That is; that although he thought you were still in the intersection you had actually passed through it before the light changed. If the officer was on a cross street he will probably testify that you ran the red because the lights had changed from red to green for his direction of traffic. Therefore, the light had to be red in your direction.

You should always time the duration of the light periods and also check to see if they are actually changing together. Some intersections are not completely synchronized because they allow for the intersection to clear of traffic, especially if the intersection is very wide or there is a heavy flow of traffic. If not, you can show the officer was in error. You can ask him on cross-examination if he actually saw the light change and if he has timed them. Always ask the question so he has to answer "yes" or "no". If he didn't see it change or doesn't know the duration you can argue that since you could and it hadn't changed by the time you left the intersection as you truthfully testified, then you are entitled to the reasonable doubt.

Watch it when you testify. Most prosecutors and judges will question you as to how far you were from the intersection when the light changed yellow, your speed, if you were slowing or accelerating and how long the yellow light was on. He usually has a chart on the bench like the one in Figure 6. This gives the average stopping distance for a car going a specific speed, including reaction time. With it he, as well as you, can figure out if you could actually have made it through the intersection. Try it. Then make sure that you have made such calculations before you testify to see what actually applies to you. You will find that the officer has probably put an estimate of your speed as well as the speed limit in that area.

An easy way to calculate if you had enough time to get through the signal is to take 1.47 (1.47 = 5280 ft/mile divided by 3600 seconds per hour) and multiply it by your speed in mph. This will give you your speed in feet per second. Then divide that answer into the distance in feet you were from the intersection when the yellow light came on. This will give you the time in seconds it took to get to the intersection. This does not take into account reaction time which is considered to average approximately 0.25 seconds. Obviously, if this number is less than the duration of the yellow light as you timed it or as the officer says it was then you were able to enter the intersection while it was still yellow. (See Figure 6 for a chart of stopping times.)

For example:

speed: 40 mph x 1.47 = 58ft/sec.

distance: 100 ft./58 = 1.72sec.

duration of light: 15 sec - 1.72 = 13.28 sec.

•**A right turn on a red light is now universally permitted unless otherwise indicated.** Mississippi, Montana, Rhode Island and Utah did not allow such a turn at the writing of this book but this may have changed, so if in doubt always check. You must come to a complete stop and signal before making the turn. It is the rolling stop and turn that gets ticketed.

•**About half of the states will allow a left turn on a red light but it must be made from a one-way street onto a one-way street, except for Washington which allows the turn to be made from a one or two-way street onto a one-way street.** Note: A flashing red light means "stop", the same as a "stop sign". A flashing yellow light means "proceed with caution".

•**Another problem traffic light is the one which has both a green go ahead light as well as a left turn only arrow.** Many people find this confusing. You have a green arrow and a green signal so you can proceed straight ahead or make a left turn. If there is only a green arrow then you may only make a left turn and may not proceed ahead. If there is just a green light, then you may proceed ahead and also make left turn when it is safe to proceed. Many accidents have occured because the motorist who get both a green arrow and a green light waits until it cycles to just a green light. The result being a rear end collision.

All states consider these violations seriously but Rhode Island seems to put special emphasis on traffic light violations by specifying in its drivers handbook that the penalty for this section is a maximum fine of $500 or one year in jail.

•**A "Yield Sign" means to allow other traffic to proceed before you merge with the traffic flow and if necessary to come to a complete stop as you would for a stop sign.** In a situation of being charged with failing to yield you will have to show that it was indeed safe for you to merge. If you wish you can use the math in Figure 7 that applies to traffic signals to calculate how much time you had to enter the flow of traffic. You can estimate the distance oncoming traffic was from you and the speed. Then figure out your own speed in merging. This can give a good idea if the merger was safe. That is; if you can testify that no traffic had to take evasive action such as changing lanes or slowing to accommodate your entry into traffic, then the merger may be considered safe, assuming that your merging speed was not excessive. There should be no "burning of tire rubber".

Remember that telling the judge how "hot" your car was does not make a failure to yield safe or legal.

•"Uncontrolled Intersections" are those where there are no lights or signs to control the flow of traffic. You must therefore know the rules. Remember, while the laws say "yield" to traffic this usually means stop until it is safe to proceed. Failure to do so is what gets you tickets.

The rules are:

°Yield if you are on a one or two lane road entering onto a multiple lane highway.

°Yield if you are on a unpaved road entering onto a paved one.

°Yield to vehicles who have or are entering the intersection from the right, unless they are far enough away to make proceeding safe.

°Yield if you are going to turn left and traffic is oncoming.

°Yield if you are entering a "T" intersection: that is; one which will require you to make a left or right turn to continue on your way.

°Yield if you are entering a roadway from a private road, alley or driveway.

°Yield to flagmen and traffic control officers or special traffic signs.

You can see that you must know in detail the rule of the road which applies if you are cited for violating one of the above. In trial, diagrams are important because if you can show that it was safe to proceed: that is; if the oncoming traffic was far enough away for you to safely proceed then what you did was legal. It is important to find out where the officer was when he made his observations, then check and see what was really visible.

•**Turns, lane changes and signaling go together.** Most states require that you give the correct signal for one hundred feet before you make the turn, or lane change. However, if there is no traffic in the immediate vicinity it is doubtful if you would be ticketed for failure to signal. If you are ticketed, then the officer will probably try to show that there was traffic close enough to be affected by your turn. Again, you must check the area to see where the officer was when he observed you, if he could see what he said he did or if his perception was off because of his location.

One other thing, if you were in fact signaling by the use of turn signals and you are stopped for not signaling, check your turn signals before the officer starts to write the ticket. If you can show that your turn signal was defective then he may let you go with a warning or merely give you a fix-it ticket. This is one of the few cases where it may be profitable to talk with the officer.

While this book was being written, the author was pulled over at night on a freeway for no apparent reason. The first thing the officer asked for, of course, was the driver's license. Needless to say I was

*polite. He then asked if I knew that my
rear lights were out?   I didn't and ex-
pressed my appreciation to him for stopping me as I knew that it was dangerous.
He suggested that I pull off the freeway
and see if I could fix them.   I thanked
him again and did so.*

**Turning movements are simple if you follow
the rules and turn from the proper lane into the clos-
est proper lane.** (See Figure 8.) The important thing
to remember is to be sure that there is enough distance between you and oncoming traffic to make a safe
turn without "peeling rubber". You will be asking for
a ticket if you don't slow down enough to make a safe
turn. If the officer sees your car swerve, fishtail, sway,
dip or oncoming traffic have to brake suddenly for
you to complete your turn you will get ticketed.

Of course, you can show that your car sways easily at slow speed because of poor shocks which you
have now replaced and/or that the officer was mistak-
en in his perception of the distance of oncoming traffic. You can question, if he says that the turn was not
safe, how far from you was oncoming traffic if any; did
anyone take evasive action or honk their horns or
give any indication that your turn was a hazard to
them; how fast was the other traffic moving? You can
figure out how much time you had to make the turn
by taking the speed and dividing it by the distance
(mph x 1.47 = feet/second). Then divide that by the
distance of the oncoming car in feet.

Turn lanes are special situations. If you find
yourself in a turn lane and you don't want to be there,
complete the turn and go around the block anyway. It
is not permissible to back up or swerve out of controlled lanes. It is easier and safer to go around.

Another special situation is a lane change on the highway to get to an off-ramp.** If you realize you are going to miss the ramp and have to make a sweeping series of lane changes across the highway to make it, don't. Go to the next off-ramp. Above all, don't stop and backup. This would be hard to justify as safe. We know that in some situations it can be several miles to the next off-ramp but consider the inconvenience in having to go to court as well as the danger.

•**Change of direction turns commonly called U-turns and "K" or "3 point" turns** are allowed in some form in all states except Vermont. All other states require that such turns only be made if they can be done without endangering other traffic. Most states have a rule which requires that there be visibility for 500 feet to approaching traffic. This distance can vary from a low of 200 feet in California to 1000 feet in Minnesota. These turns are not allowed on hills, curves, interstate or limited access highways or where prohibited by ordinance or signs. You will know it is permitted to make such a turn if there is a posted sign, otherwise you had better study the law of your state as well as your city.

Some states have very specific rules governing where a U-turn may be made and also allow individual cities to enact their own laws limiting such activity. For instance, in New York State change of direction turns are allowed except in New York City even if there are no posted signs prohibiting the turns. California does not permit a U-turn in a business district except at an intersection, or on a divided highway where an opening has been provided but permits such a turn in a residence district only if approaching vehicles are 200 or more feet away or at a controlled intersection.

The defense in such change of direction cases requires that you examine each law for the individual elements and then try to raise a doubt that one of those elements is missing. For example; that you were not in a business district, that there was no vehicle approaching you or that the vehicle was beyond the specified distance.

•**Passing is usually prohibited on hills, curves, bridges, tunnels, school zones and to the right of vehicles in the same lane unless there is a lane or the vehicle is making a left turn and it is clear and safe to pass.** In addition, passing may be controlled by the use of marked lanes. All states prohibit passing or crossing over a double solid yellow set of lines. If one line is broken on your side with a solid line on the far side then passing is permitted, if safe. If there is a lane created by solid yellow and broken lines this can only be used for turning or for passing, not travelling. So if you use this lane for passing, complete the movement and get back to the right. Don't forget to signal.

•**Following too close or "tailgating" is universally prohibited.** All states recommend that you kept at least 1 to 1 1/2 car lengths behind the car in front of you for every 10 miles per hour of speed. Some suggest you use a "two-second" rule. Namely that you keep your vehicle two seconds behind the front vehicle which will give you about a 1 1/2 car length interval. You do this by picking a checkpoint and as the end of the car ahead passes it start counting until your car reaches that point. If it takes two or more seconds to reach the same point you are at a reasonably safe distance. Obviously the greater the distance the safer.

•**Bicyclists are also governed by the rules of the road applicable to motor vehicles.** Usually, violations will not be reported to the local DMV. Lately some states like California are increasing penalties for bicycle violations such as DUI.

•**Pedestrians** must also obey traffic signs plus any special ones governing them.   Jaywalking, or crossing the street other than in a crosswalk or intersection is usually not allowed in business districts.   Of course, if there are no designated crosswalks you may cross anywhere as long as it is safe to do so.

In addition where you are crossing with a "walk-don't walk"signal it is possible to get a ticket for crossing against instructions.   However, if you can show that you started to cross when it was proper and the signal changed on you before you were safely across the street you will not have committed a violation.   In this type of case it is important to time the duration of the pedestrian signals as well as the traffic signals.   You may also check with the highway department to see if any complaints or repairs have been made to that set of signals.

Also where a motorist may enter an intersection on a yellow traffic light, in most states a pedestrian must not do so.

Pedestrians have a duty to yield to traffic as well as motorists.   Just remember, a pedestrian who insists on his right away may end up dead.

Each state varies on its "hitchhiking" laws and if that is your means of transportation, be careful to know what you are doing ahead of time.   If you are hitchhiking improperly you can get arrested.

For example Tennessee makes it "illegal to stand in the street to solicit a ride."

•**Parking tickets** are the universal pain in the neck.   They are one of the main money makers for cities and towns because most people simply pay them.

Failure to pay such tickets will not, usually, result in warrants for your arrest since you have not signed them as "promises to appear" but a failure to pay will prevent your being able to register your car when renewal time comes up in many states or you may become the victim of the dreaded **"Denver Boot"**. This is a device which is attached to your wheel and immobilizes the car. You have to pay up to get it removed. Whatever you do do not try to tamper with the "boot" as that will carry a separate penalty.

You can win these tickets by setting them for trial. It is rare that the ticket giver will show up. If she does show up she will have to testify that she remembers writing your particular ticket and if she cannot do so you may win. Lastly, an element that must be proved is that you own the car. If that cannot be done by official records you win, unless of course you came up to the car when the ticket was being written and admitted that you had parked it there. Don't testify if you are going to supply those answers.

If all the above fail and you are positive that you were not illegally parked proceed with trial as in any other moving violation. You can show that the area was not properly marked, that the ticket writer was too eager and wrote the ticket before the time limit had expired and/or that the parking ordinance was illegal or unconstitutional in itself.

The "Never There" parking ticket is a different matter. This occurs when you find out that you cannot register your car or you get a notice of intent to issue a warrant because of an unpaid parking ticket and you know that you were never there to get the ticket and hadn't loaned your car to someone else. This may happen due to an error by the ticket giver in writing down your vehicle identification or errors made in entering the data into the computers. Your state may have a law like the one that went into effect in California January 1986 which requires that both the ticket and the notice indicate the time, date and location of the violation, license number and expiration date, color, make and model and year of the vehicle. To defend against this type of ticket you have to get a copy of the original ticket from the issuing agency or the court. If you do not receive a copy within fifteen days of your request the ticket must be dismissed. Therefore, you must be sure to make your request in writing, keeping a copy, and send it by certified mail, return receipt requested, so that you can prove that you sent the request and that it was received.

Once you receive the copy of the ticket check your license number against what is written there. If it is correct then check for any description of the vehicle on the ticket against your car; such as make, type and color. This information will also be on your registration. If the description does not match then you can request a court appearance and trial. The California law allows you to request, in writing, that the ticket be dismissed. Be sure to enclose a copy of your vehicle registration.

If the prosecution or the judge refuses to dismiss your case, you will then have to go to court. You will have to show why your vehicle is not the one listed on the citation. You can do this by witness or business records such as a time card or sign in sheet showing that you were someplace else at the date and time of the ticket.

Some courts may permit a trial in writing if you live too far away from the court. If you chose to use this route then set forth your reasoning in as orderly and logical a manner as possible including copies of your employment records and/or notarized statements of your witnesses. If you lose you may still be able to request a regular trial. If all this does not work then you will have to pay up. If you are getting many such tickets and it really is not your car getting cited then it is possible that there is another vehicle which is too similar to yours in description and license number. A less drastic solution to this problem than selling your car may be to get your license plates changed.

Do not ignore these tickets. That can land you in jail just as well as any of the other violations.

CHAPTER 13

DRIVING UNDER THE INFLUENCE

Driving While Under The Influence of Alcohol and/or Drugs (commonly called DUI, DWI or drunk driving) is probably the most serious of all the driving offenses. If there are injuries or death to anyone other than yourself you will be facing felony charges and state prison.

A common statement from people arrested for DUI is that "I was not drunk!" You do not have to be drunk to be arrested and convicted for DUI. That is why the crime is actually called driving under the influence and NOT drunk driving. The term, "drunk driving", is merely a shorthand way of saying driving while under the influence. The initials "DUI" or "DWI" are more accurate.

Driving Under the Influence is a serious crime for the obvious reason that an automobile that is not being controlled properly is a danger to everyone with the occurrence of injury to property, person and even death being all too common.

It is serious for you, the defendant, because of the penalties which you face. For example: jail, loss of driving privilege, large fines, increased or cancelled automobile insurance or civil law suits. In addition, there is an increasingly hostile atmosphere toward drunk drivers. This makes it harder to get a fair trial with a fair jury and makes leniency by the court less frequent.

There are so many important technicalities to a DUI trial where the issues involve the picking of a jury, the accuracy of chemical tests, the cross-examination of expert witnesses, the evaluation of your story and how much you had to drink, prior convictions, etc., that it is strongly urged that you retain the services of a lawyer.

An arrest for driving while under the influence is quite a bit different from an ordinary traffic stop. *The minute the officer detects what he thinks are the symptoms of some kind of intoxication, the way he handles the situation changes..* You will be questioned more carefully, speech patterns will be noted, he will be checking your eyes, watching while you go through your wallet looking for your driver's license, etc. Breath odor of alcoholic beverages may be the first tip off. Peanuts may help absorb this odor but they won't help if your driving is erratic and your balance is bad.

The officer's attitude may also change. You may be faced with hostility, sarcasm, and rudeness. Your attitude during this time is critical. Stay calm, polite and PAY ATTENTION. You will be asked to perform as series of tests the outcome of which may determine if you are going to be arrested.

A common police report will read like the following: "While talking with the suspect I detected the odor of an alcoholic beverage (alcohol itself is odorless). I noticed that the suspect's eyes were bloodshot and watery and his speech was slow and slurred. He fumbled through his wallet, passing his license several times. I ordered him to get out of the car and proceed to the sidewalk (or between cars) to administer some field sobriety tests. The suspect had to use the car to maintain his balance. He staggered and swayed as he walked to the sidewalk. I then explained and demonstrated several field sobriety tests which he attempted and failed. Based on his driving, physical symptoms and performance on the field sobriety tests I felt that he had been driving under the influence of alcohol." It is almost comical to realize that most police reports will read this way. A checklist style report may be used along with narrative style report. (See Figure 10.)

The field sobriety tests (FST's) that are administered are usually taken from among the following tests:

•**The Heel to Toe Test** in which you are required to walk a certain number of steps on an imaginary or real straight line, placing the heel of one foot to the toe of the other, then turning around and returning. You may be asked to walk a certain number of steps in one direction and a different number back. There is a trick to this test which is let your foot fall back against the toe of the other foot. It is much harder if you try deliberately to place it against the toe.

•**The Leg Lift Test** in which you are told to lift one foot in front of you off the ground a certain height and hold it there. You may be told to hold your foot up for a certain time or the officer will note how long you can hold your foot in the air.

•**The Finger to Nose Test** in which you are told to hold your arms out to the side with the index finger extended. Close your eyes and place your head back. You are to then touch the tip of your index finger to the tip of your nose. The trick here is to be sure to keep your arm straight and only bend at the elbow, you should arrive at the tip of the nose most of the time.

•**The Finger Count Test** in which you are to touch, with your thumb the fingers on the same hand in order and then backwards, starting with either the little finger or index per instructions-1,2,3,4-4,3,2,1 and repeat.

•**The Balance Test** in which you are to simply stand with your head back and eyes closed to see if your body sways and how far it sways from center.

•**The Alphabet Test** in which you will be asked to recite the alphabet. The smart officers will have you write it down. This may be combined with having you do numbers backwards from 100.

•**The Pick Up Test** will consists of you being asked to pick up coins of various denominations from the ground.

•**The Nystagmus Test** is a fairly recent test of dubious value but is being more commonly used. The officer will hold his finger or a pencil in front of your face about a foot away and move it to the side and up and down having you follow the movement with your eyes keeping your head motionless, first one direction then the other. At a certain distance to the side he may observe the eyeball to have a slight bounce. This side to side movement is called horizontal nystagmus. Vertical nystagmus is tested in the same manner only moving the object up and down. It is felt by some experts that measuring the degree of onset of nystagmus; that is, when the eye starts to bounce, will allow the officer to make a correlation to the amount of blood-alcohol in the system. This conclusion has not been accepted in most jurisdictions.

The officer will usually have a fellow officer witness these tests and one of them will demonstrate the tests. It is a good idea if you have someone with you to ask them to watch. However, it is not unusual for you to be separated from your witnesses in such a manner that it is difficult for them to see.

You should be most observant, if possible, to see if there are any witnesses around the area who are watching as they can be quite helpful if in fact you are not under the influence.

If the officer feels that you are under the influence you will probably be arrested, handcuffed and taken in for some form of a chemical test.

Performance on these tests can be improved by practice. In other words, if you are experienced in performing the tests then you will do better on them even if intoxicated.

> *This writer attended a demonstration at the Los Angeles Police Academy several years ago in which, while most of us ate dinner, others were being given drinks at measured intervals followed by a series of FST's. It was interesting to watch some of the test subjects do better and better on the FST's as they drank more and more.*

If you ask the officer how you did on the tests, you will probably get a noncommittal answer or even "fine". If you are being handcuffed, do not believe it or count on such an answer as a defense, it is said simply to ensure your cooperation.

Implied consent laws exist in all states. It is a requirement for the issuance of your driver's license that, upon a proper traffic stop with a belief that you may be under the influence of either alcohol or drugs, you must take a chemical test to determine the amount of alcohol or drugs in your system. You are usually not allowed to consult with a lawyer in order to make up your mind as to which test you wish to take. Refusal to take or to complete one of the chemical tests can be used at trial to show a "consciousness of guilt". That is, you didn't take the test because you knew that you were too intoxicated. It will also result in your privilege to drive being suspended. (See Chapter 17—Licensing.) A refusal can also result in a stiffer penalty. In California, for example, a refusal will result in a mandatory forty-eight hours in jail.

There are three types of chemical tests that are commonly administered:

•**The Breath Test** requires you to blow into some kind of a measuring machine, of which there are several types. The machine will give a reading showing the amount of alcohol in your system. The problem with these tests is that some machines are subject to mishandling by the police officers. "Dial a Duce" was a common term to describe this action. The newer machines were designed to minimize handling by the officer to eliminate this accusation.

The officers prefer breath tests because they can be easily administered at the police station. You may be told to take this test and if it is low enough you will be released. This is not necessarily true. If you agree you should be sure to insist that if the test is too high you want a blood test. This test is only for alcohol. However, if the results are .00% or too low to jibe with your symptoms of intoxication you may be asked to take one of the other two tests. A refusal to take a second test can be used against you in court but if you have taken the breath test, it is doubtful that your privilege to drive can be suspended as the law usually only requires that you submit to one test.

•**The Urine Test** requires you to give two urine samples twenty minutes apart. The first sample will be discarded, because it would show too much alcohol to be correlated with that in your blood stream. The second sample will be kept and analyzed. The sample can also be tested for the presence of drugs. The urine test is not considered as accurate a test as the blood test for alcohol because it is based on the assumption that one's body will empty into the bladder the same quantity of alcohol from the liver each time. In addition, the bladder will accumulate urine over a period of time and does not reflect the body condition at any particular time. Plus there is no way to be sure that the bladder has been emptied the first time. This is the least accurate of the tests and is the most attackable from a trial viewpoint. If you have had a lot to drink, this might be the best test to request.

• **The Blood Test** is usually administered by a third party, a licensed nurse, technician or doctor who is not a member of the police department. Hopefully, they will be more impartial than the officers. They may also be witnesses for you as to your state of sobriety at the time of the test. The skin should be cleansed with a non-alcohol solution such as Zephiran or Betadine. If alcohol is used, it will contaminate the sample. Therefore, you should ask what is being used. The sample should be immediately refrigerated and tested as soon as possible as blood will break down and ferment (change into alcohol) somewhat itself. A preservative is supposed to be in the test vial.

A problem here is that it is customary to turn the sample back over to the officer who will then enter it into evidence, hopefully refrigerated. He should then have it analyzed. However, a too common practice is not to have the sample tested until after a not guilty plea has been entered at arraignment and the case set for pretrial or trial. As this can be weeks or months later, the accuracy of the test can suffer. This test can also be used for determining the presence of drugs in the system, although the urine test is preferred for drug testing.

In California and elsewhere you are entitled to a second test, if you have taken a breath test. This is usually a blood test. The test may be at county expense or at your own expense. It is a good idea to make such a request. If refused, you should obtain a test as soon as you get out of jail, assuming that your release is within six to eight hours after your last drink. Remember, alcohol is excreted by your body at an approximate rate of 0.02% per hour. If you are accused of being under the influence of drugs, a urine sample taken up to 72 hours after arrest may provide a helpful test, if negative.

The analysis of blood or urine for drugs is only done to determine the presence of the drugs not how much of the drug was present in your system. This is where the services of your lawyer can be helpful, especially while you are still in jail, as he can make the necessary arrangements to get a properly licensed individual to the jail to administer the test to you.

Obviously, if you are loaded, forget it. The above suggestions won't help.

The best advice this writer can give is: "If you have been drinking, DON'T DRIVE."

It is not illegal to have something to drink and to drive thereafter. It is only when the alcohol effects the manner in which you drive, that it becomes illegal. You do not have to be "drunk" to be "under the influence". If you are going to drink and drive you should be aware of how alcohol enters and leaves your system. The usual way alcohol is ingested is by drinking.

Alcohol goes into your system extremely fast and leaves it extremely slowly. For example, it takes about one hour to eliminate the alcohol of one standard drink. *If you have had two drinks within one hour then you should wait for at least two hours before you drive, and so on.* Obviously, there really is no such thing as a standard drink. These factors vary with the actual amount of alcohol in the drink, the time over which it was drunk, your weight, health and physical condition.

Pacing yourself is a good way to avoid trouble if you are going to drink and drive. That is, to limit your number of drinks and spread out the drinking of each drink over a substantial period of time. It also helps to consider diluting your drinks. (Figure 9 will give you an idea of what the percentages of blood alcohol mean in relation to what you have had to drink.) Obviously, if you are drinking to get drunk this advice is not for you. Just don't drive.

Driving with too much alcohol in your system is a separate crime from DUI. It exists in many states like California. It is driving with a certain amount of alcohol in your system or higher (BAC = blood alcohol content). What this means is that if the results of your blood test show that the amount of alcohol in your system is that specified amount or higher (0.10% blood-alcohol in California) you will have committed a crime regardless of the effect it had upon your driving. This means that the prosecution only has to prove that you were driving the car and had the specified amount of alcohol in your system or higher. Erratic or good driving, how well you did or did not do on the field sobriety test, none of these things are important.

Most states use the figure of 0.10% as a presumption of driving under the influence and as the new limit for the crime of driving with too high a blood alcohol level. Maine brags about how strict its enforcement of the DUI law is in its Driver's handbook. Two states; Alaska and Indiana and Washington, D.C.; use levels of .05%. Michigan and New York use a level of .07% and Utah uses .08%. A person 20 years or less in Maine with a BAC of .02% will lose his license for one year without a court proceeding. These amounts may be changed so if you drink and drive it would be a good idea to find out what levels of blood alcohol are used by your state. This can easily be found out from the traffic law book, the DMV, your lawyer or the police.

There are instruments available on the market, which measure your breath and will give you an approximate breath alcohol (BAC) level. They are pocket sized and inexpensive and if you are a regular drinker would probably be a good investment. But use such an instrument with caution as it is not as accurate as the machine the police will use and does not measure the effect the alcohol will have on you. It can only be used as a guide.

Prior convictions or simply "Priors" are one other aspect of driving under the influence of which you must be aware. This term means that each offense that you accumulate within a specific time   period (seven years in California) will result in heavier and heavier penalties. For example, in California, a third conviction of driving under the influence within seven years will result in a mandatory one hundred and twenty days in jail plus a three year revocation of the privilege to drive plus a one year alcohol program and a minimum fine of $691 including the penalty assessment.

Prior convictions may be attacked by a knowledgeable attorney for constitutional problems. That is, when you were convicted of the prior offense something may not have been done properly during the court proceeding which will prevent that conviction from being used against you. This will usually deal with whether you were properly advised of your constitutional rights and if, after being so advised, you knowingly, intelligently and voluntarily gave up those rights to enter a plea. If the record shows that you were not advised of or did not give up the right to counsel and/or jury trial, then the prior conviction is probably not useable. However, if you were represented by an attorney, then it is presumed that you were properly advised. This is one of the first things an attorney will check.

You can save yourself some time and money by obtaining a copy of the prior conviction so that it can be reviewed by your attorney. All you have to do is go to the clerk of the court where you were convicted and ask for a "certified copy" of the court record of the prior. There is a fee for such a copy, which may be waived if you can prove that you are indigent. Be aware that if you have been placed on probation for your previous conviction and are still on that probation, requesting the court papers may let that court know that you have a new arrest which may result in your having to face a violation of that court's probation.

Plea bargaining may be attempted by trying to get lesser penalties or your DUI charge reduced to a less serious misdemeanor such as reckless driving, or even to a lesser infraction, as speeding. This procedure is possible in most jurisdictions if your blood alcohol is low or right at the minimum presumptive level. It also helps if your driving was not too bad and your performance on the field sobriety tests was respectable. In order to achieve this type of charge reduction the prosecution must be persuaded that there is something wrong with their case. Or if you can show that your living depends upon your driving the prosecution might agree to the reduction. It never hurts to ask the prosecutor. If the prosecutor won't agree to reduce the charge there is the possibility that the judge may agree to reduce the penalties, if possible. The judge can be asked for an indicated sentence or a lower sentence from what had earlier been indicated.

The use of a Private Investigator can be helpful
in these cases.   He can trace your steps during the
time period preceding your arrest to validate your
statement as to the amount of drinking you actually
did do and the effect it had upon you by locating witnesses who can verify your statements.

We have not gone into how the various chemical tests work or how a DUI trial is conducted in detail
since it is felt that it is foolhardy to attempt to represent yourself in such a trial.

However, if you are going to represent yourself, it is suggested that you study *Defense of Drunk
Driving Cases* by Richard Erwin, Mathew Bender,
1966. It is the most complete book on the subject. The
book will give examples of direct and cross-
examination. It covers all the tests that are presently
used and will cover the law of each state. It is difficult
to read and understand. It can probably be found in
most complete law libraries.

The best advice this writer can give you is, as
mentioned before, See a lawyer. If you have been
drinking, Don't Drive. If you have to drink, take sufficient money to take a cab home, pace yourself and be
prepared and willing to wait a sufficient time after
your last drink to let the effects wear off. Finally, you
can use a technique used in Europe where the laws are
even rougher than here. That is, go in a group and
have a *"designated nondrinker-driver"* then switch
the next time out.

A conviction or even an acquittal of the charge
of Driving Under the Influence will be the most expensive set of drinks you will ever have.

KNOW YOUR LIMIT

NUMBER OF DRINKS IN ONE HOUR

APPROXIMATE BLOOD ALCOHOL CONTENT (BAC)

DRINKS	PER	BODY WEIGHT IN POUNDS						
	100	120	140	160	180	200	220	240
1	0.04	0.03	0.02	0.02	0.02	0.02	0.02	0.02
2	0.06	0.06	0.05	0.05	0.04	0.04	0.03	0.03
3	0.11	0.09	0.08	0.07	0.06	0.06	0.05	0.05
4	0.15	0.12	0.11	0.09	0.08	0.08	0.07	0.06
5	0.19	0.16	0.13	0.12	0.11	0.09	0.09	0.08
6	0.23	0.19	0.16	0.14	0.13	0.11	0.10	0.09
7	0.30	0.22	0.19	0.16	0.15	0.13	0.12	0.11
8	0.38	0.25	0.21	0.19	0.17	0.15	0.14	0.13
9	0.34	0.28	0.24	0.21	0.19	0.17	0.15	0.14
10	0.38	0.31	0.27	0.23	0.21	0.19	0.17	0.16

1 Drink = 86 proof 1.5 oz. whiskey, gin, etc.:
1beer (12oz.): 3 oz. wine (20%) or 5 oz. wine (12%).

Subtract 0.1% for each hour of drinking.

BE SAFE: Wait One Hour For Each Drink Consumed.

0.08% BAC is illegal in Utah and other States.
0.10% BAC is illegal in ALL States.

BLOOD ALCOHOL CONTENTS

FIGURE 9

LOCATION		**P.D. DUI**	DR#	
TIME & DATE	RD.	**ARREST REPORT**	BOOKING NO.	
			CHARGES	

| SUSP NAME | LAST | FIRST | MIDDLE | D.O.B. | DRIVERS LIC NUMBER | STATE |

EYES: ☐ Apparently Normal ☐ Watery ☐ Bloodshot ☐ Sleepy Eyelids ☐ Other

PUPILS: ☐ Apparently Normal ☐ Constricted ☐ Dilated ☐ Poor Reaction to Light ☐ Other

FACE: ☐ Apparently Normal ☐ Flushed ☐ Pale ☐ Sweaty ☐ Other

SPEECH: ☐ Apparently Normal ☐ Slurred ☐ Stuttering ☐ Incoherent ☐ Fair ☐ Confused ☐ Clear & Correct Enunciation ☐ Other

BREATH: ☐ Odor of Alcoholic Beverage ☐ None ☐ Faint ☐ Moderate ☐ Strong ☐ Other

EXITING VEHICLE: ☐ Sure ☐ Unstable ☐ Lost Balance ☐ Used Vehicle to Maintain Balance ☐ Falling ☐ Other

WALKING: ☐ Apparently Normal ☐ Unsteady ☐ Swaying ☐ Staggering ☐ Falling ☐ Needed Assistance ☐ Other

TURNING: ☐ Apparently Normal ☐ Hesitant ☐ Losing Balance ☐ Swaying ☐ Falling ☐ Needed Assistance ☐ Other

STATIONARY POSITION: ☐ Apparently Normal ☐ Swaying ☐ Sagging Knees ☐ Falling ☐ Other

		What Have You Been Drinking		How Much
Sick or Injured	☐ Yes ☐ No			
Diabetic or Epileptic	☐ Yes ☐ No	Time of Last Drink & Amount		
Do You Take Insulin	☐ Yes ☐ No			
Under Care of Doctor or Dentist	☐ Yes ☐ No	Where Were You Going	What Time is it	Actual Time
Using Medicine or Drugs	☐ Yes ☐ No			
Do You Have Any Physical Defects	☐ Yes ☐ No	Time Started Drinking?		Frequency of Drinks
Explain "Yes" Answers Below:				

ALPHABET
☐ Sure, Correct
☐ Slow, Hesitant
☐ Skipping Letters (indicate)

_____
☐ Started Over ( ) Times
☐ Slurred
☐ Not Understandable
☐ Too Slow
☐ Slow, Deliberate

DIGITAL COUNT
☐ Sure, Correct ☐ Slow, Deliberate
☐ Slurred ☐ Confused
☐ Slow Hesitant ☐ Added Numbers
☐ Interchanged ☐ Not as Instructed
Fingers ☐ Improper Count
☐ Other

Where Are You Now _____ Actual Loc. _____

When & What Had to Eat? _____

NOTE: Avoid any unnecessary time delay between F.S.T. and intoxilyzer.

Advised Miranda? ☐ Yes ☐ No

MODIFIED BALANCE
☐ Apparently Normal
☐ Swaying (explain)
☐ Leaning (explain)
☐ Feet Separation
☐ Other
EXPLAIN: _____

ONE LEG STANCE
LEFT / RIGHT
☐ ☐ Sure
☐ ☐ Hesitant
☐ ☐ Used Arms for Balance
☐ ☐ Lost Balance
☐ ☐ Falling
☐ ☐ Other
EXPLAIN_____

HEEL-TO-TOE WALK
Explain:
△ - LEFT FOOT O - RIGHT FOOT Balance, Walking & Turning

ABILITY TO RETAIN AND FOLLOW SIMPLE INSTRUCTIONS:
☐ Good Retention and Quick Response to Instruction ☐ Fair Retention and Response ☐ Poor Retention and Response ☐ Nuisance ☐ Interrupting
☐ Evasive Questions ☐ Attempts Tests Before/During Instructions ☐ Other

UNUSUAL ACTIONS OF SUSPECT: ☐ Hiccoughing ☐ Burping ☐ Vomiting ☐ Fighting ☐ Crying ☐ Laughing ☐ Defecating

_____
_____
_____
_____

CHEMICAL TESTS:
BLOOD: _____ DATE: _____ TIME: _____ LOCATION: _____ BY: _____
BREATH: _____ DATE: _____ TIME: _____ LOCATION: _____ BY: _____ RESULTS: _____
URINE: _____ DATE: _____ TIME NO. 1 _____ TIME NO. 2 _____ LOCATION _____ BY: _____
REFUSAL ☐ Yes ☐ No. ADVISED OF 13353 V.C. ☐ Yes ☐ No TIME: _____ LOCATION: _____ BY: _____

PPD 266

ARREST REPORT

FIGURE 10

CHAPTER 14

OTHER CRIMES

There are other serious traffic crimes besides Driving under the Influence, all of which carry very real and possible jail sentences. **Such crimes are: Reckless Driving; Hit and Run; Exhibition of Speed; Speed Contest; Driving without a License; Driving while your Privilege to Drive is Suspended or Revoked; etc..** *In all of these types of cases it is felt that the assistance of a lawyer is vital.* At least, consult a lawyer before deciding to represent yourself.

Whether you decide to represent yourself or to hire a lawyer there are several things that you can do to help yourself.

If you don't have a driver's license, GET ONE! Judges do not look very favorably on anyone driving without a license. It is a separate crime which is covered in Chapter 17—Licensing. Obtaining your license is a powerful gesture to show the court that you are serious in obeying the law.

Fix your car. If you have equipment problems, fix the car and keep the receipts. If you fix it yourself, keep the receipts for necessary parts having the parts house fill out the name of the part in addition to the part number.

If you are unable to get the car fixed, for whatever reason, you may be able to bring the license plates to the court, being sure that the vehicle is parked off the street. You may, sometimes, leave the plates with the court until you can get the vehicle fixed. If you do this, the court will usually accept the plates instead of a fine.

If you have been in an accident, take photos of the vehicle before you have the vehicle repaired and then take photos after the repair.

•Be sure to report the accident to your insurance company and be especially sure that the accident is reported to the DMV. Some states require that the local police be notified of the accident also, assuming that they were not called to the scene of the accident. Failure to make a such a report can result in your privilege to drive being suspended.

•Settle the damages very carefully. Report accidents to your insurance company and let them handle it. Make no admission of fault. Notify your lawyer. Your statements to your lawyer as to what happened are confidential and cannot be discovered. Statements made in order to comply with a law requiring you to report the accident are not usable in court. Statements you make to the victims or witnesses of an accident CAN be used against you in court and these people may be hostile, even to the point of doing you harm. Let your lawyer or your insurance company do the negotiations so you can avoid contact with the "victims" of your accident. If you are not insured, and do not wish to use a lawyer, at least let a third party do the negotiations.

•REMEMBER, if you are in an accident, don't admit being at fault. A common failing that many people have is to say, "I am sorry". This can be and is taken as an admission of guilt and not sympathy. If questioned by the police insist on your right to a lawyer before being questioned. They usually will not try to question you.

•In cases where you are required to report an accident including a statement of what happened, the state law usually has a provision that prohibits such a statement from being used against you in a criminal or civil action.

•Gather the names, addresses and phone numbers of witnesses. It is better to have a professional obtain a statement from the witnesses as soon as possible. If you obtain the services of a lawyer he will probably use the services of an investigator. The police may have already gathered this information and put it into a accident report. But except in unusual cases, they will not try to find other witnesses.

•Obtain the police and accident report. This is done by going to the police station and asking the man at the desk. He will need to know the date and location of the accident. There is usually a copying fee. If they say they will only turn the items over to your lawyer, tell them that you are representing yourself. If that doesn't work, you will have to wait until you hire an attorney or go to court.   In court, after you have either entered a not guilty plea or asked for more time to enter a plea, you ask for a copy of the complaint which is the paper formally charging you with the crime and copies of the reports.

•In requesting time to enter a plea so that you can consult an attorney, you are in fact asking for a continuance of your case. The judge will ask you to "waive time". This means he is asking you to give up your right to a speedy trial because you are asking for more time. In these serious cases time can be an advantage so that the case can be properly prepared. So do not worry about agreeing to waive time. It is very rare that the arresting officer fails to show up for one of these cases. Since you now know ahead of time what to expect, you can see why early consultation with a lawyer is important.

•Prepare your own written statement as soon as possible after the incident as discussed in Chapter 3— Getting the Ticket.

Following the above steps can make things a little easier for you in preparing to face the charges and may help in reducing the fees a lawyer will have to charge you to do the same work.

If you decide to represent yourself in these more serious cases the following discussion will help you to understand the nature and elements of the crimes and how to prepare the case for court.

Reckless Driving is a crime that usually requires a showing by the officer that you were driving upon a highway in willful and wanton disregard for the safety of persons or property.

Many officers will wait until they have observed at least three consecutive violations of the traffic law before writing such a ticket. However, if they consider the one violation observed to be in and of itself reckless, they will ticket you. For example, speed of 100+ mph on city streets can be considered reckless driving as well as speeding.

Reckless Driving is viewed very seriously. If you have been stopped and told this is the crime you are going to be charged with be especially polite and cooperative without admitting anything. A "smart mouth" here will get you taken to jail.

If you decide to fight the charge, a jury trial, to which you are entitled, is the only way to go. Remember, also, that if you can't hire an attorney you are entitled to appointed counsel. If you are representing yourself you will have to treat each moving violation separately to show why the officer was mistaken, and further that there was no danger to others. This can be shown by a careful investigation of the area in which you where driving. Weather, road and traffic conditions are very important.

The charge of Reckless Driving is often used as part of a plea bargain, wherein you may be originally charged with Driving Under the Influence but are allowed to plead to this as a lesser charge. It is lesser because it doesn't carry the mandatory penalties and restrictions which a DUI will carry. In California, however, if the charge is reduced in such a manner, it may still be used to increase the penalties if you get another DUI arrest; that is, it can be used as a "prior". (See Chapter 13—Driving Under The Influence.)

Speed Contests are when two or more vehicles engage in a course of action that can be viewed as a race on a public highway; side by side rapid acceleration or high speed driving.

The more traffic or pedestrians in the vicinity the more serious the court will treat the matter.

You might be able to plead down to a less serious infraction such as speeding depending on the circumstances and your attitude.

The officer is not required to have arrested all the drivers. In fact, you do not have to have been driving to get nailed for this charge. You may have "aided and abetted" the drivers by setting up the race, assisting or encouraging them. This type of arrest is more commonly made where there are regular "street drags" being set up. If you are there watching you could get arrested. But it has to be proved that you were actively involved in aiding or encouraging the crime.

Exhibition of Speed is the displaying of speed on a public highway. This can be done by fast driving or rapid acceleration which is usually shown by the squealing of tires or burning rubber.

This crime requires that you thought someone was watching. Strangers will do and it does not matter if they saw you.

Remember that this can be plead down to speeding or an unsafe lane change if the prosecutor will agree.

If you go to trial remember that any car can be driven so as to burn rubber. DON'T brag about your car. It is funny listening to someone say that his car couldn't possibly accelerate like that or burn rubber and upon questioning describe tremendous horsepower, special driveshafts, valve arrangements; in short, a race car in street clothes.

Hit and Run is a crime that occurs if you leave the scene of a accident without stopping and/or identifying yourself.

The elements of the crimes are: that there have been an accident to person or property such that you had notice of the damage and that you left the scene without stopping to identify yourself and render aid. The duty to stop, identify and, where there are injuries, to render aid is specified in detail in the law and is usually required knowledge to obtaining a driver's license.

It is not required that you be at fault in the accident. Merely that you not stop and identify. Fear is no excuse.

Moving your vehicle to a safe place and then returning to the scene would not be considered a violation unless the safe place was your garage in the next town and your return much later. However, an immediate stop is the best action to take.

If no one was present during the accident, such as hitting a parked car, a fence or other property, you are still required to stop and leave a statement of what happened on the car or the property along with identifying information such as your name, address and driver's license number. You must also notify the police thereafter.

This activity was made a crime to facilitate civil responsibility.

One technique that may work to get the case dismissed is what is called "civil compromise". This means that the "victim" of the crime may make a statement, usually to the judge, that you have paid for the damages and he does not wish to prosecute the case.

This is not a sure fire technique because the actual victim in this crime is the state, not the owner of the property. However, it may work. If you were responsible for the accident, then your paying it off will be required anyway. So, if the civil compromise is not accepted, the fact of your settlement will be in your favor. Be sure, when you make your payment, that you get a receipt and a release from any other damages. Check with your lawyer.

Failure to Appear is a crime which may escalate a no jail offense into a misdemeanor with a likely possibility of a jail sentence. It can also result in the suspension of your license. If your failure to appear was due to circumstances beyond your control and you came to court as soon as possible you can probably win such a charge. However, as mentioned before, if the prosecuting attorney will not agree to dismiss, then a jury trial is usually the way to go. Most judges have "heard 'em all" and will not believe your excuse. This charge is usually in company with the underlying traffic offense. On a plea of guilty to the failure to appear the other charges may be dismissed. This prevents

them from going on your record and may be important for your driving privilege. This can be negotiated
with the prosecuting attorney prior to entering the
plea.

**Failure to Pay Your Fine will also escalate a no
jail situation into jail.** *It requires that you willfully
fail to pay.* You cannot be jailed if you are financially
unable to pay your fine and can prove it. (See Chapter
16—Punishment.)

•Contempt of Court is willfully disobeying a
specific court order. This too is a misdemeanor and
can land you in jail. (See APPENDIX C—Contempt.)

•Prior Offenses: As mentioned before if you get
enough convictions of the same or similar offenses
(usually three or more) the prosecution may charge
you with a misdemeanor instead of a infraction. This
is rare as the prosecutors really do not wish to bother
with them unless your record is really bad. On the
other hand, you may demand that the infraction be
raised to a misdemeanor. By so doing you get the
right to counsel and a jury trial. You also get the
judge and prosecution mad. If you lose you are now
facing a much stiffer fine as well as a jail sentence.
Such a course of action is not recommended.

**"Strict Liability" laws are those which hold you
responsible regardless of your actions.** For example,
you would be responsible for a parking ticket that you
knew nothing about because you had lent your car to
someone else for the day. Equipment and registration
violations are similar even if you were driving someone else's car. You are guilty of the crime though you
did not intend to violate the law. Fortunately, there
are not too many of these types of laws.

As you can see from the above discussion it is
easy to avoid these problems. However, if you find

yourself in such trouble it is wise to use the services of a lawyer. If you wish to represent yourself or just be able to follow what is happening, do as suggested in the beginning of "Traffic Court" and get a copy of the law governing your situation.

Each crime, however large or small, consists of specific elements, each of which must be proved in order for there to be a conviction. These elements will be listed in the law books. Make a list of each element and number each one. Then you can then see how your individual case fits in and make a decision as to how to proceed.

Remember many cases can be won because of a combination of critical examination of each element of the crime with good investigation.

For example, a pro per defendant in Illinois beat a speeding ticket by showing the judge that the traffic signs in the town where he was stopped, O'Fallon, did not meet the standards set forth in the Illinois Motor Vehicle Code. The signs were too small. Also, they did not give proper warning that the driver was entering a town and required a more than 10 mph decrease in speed. Measurement, investigation and checking each element won.

You can see that a technical defense can win a case as well as a "I didn't do it" defense.

1

2 John Doe
   700 Main Street
3 Anywhere, CA 900XX
   (712) 891-55ZZ
4 In Propria Persona

5

6   MUNICIPAL COURT OF THE ANYWHERE JUDICAL DISTRICT
7   COUNTY OF LOS ANGELES, STATE OF CALIFORNIA

8 PEOPLE OF THE STATE OF CALIFORNIA)   Case #M684930
                           Plaintiff,)   Affidavit of Prejudice
9   )
)
           vs.   )
10   )
)
           JOHN DOE   )
11   )
                       Defendant.   )

12 ─────────────────────────────────────

13 John Doe declares as follows: That he is a party to the within pro-

14 ceedings. That the Honorable John Jurist, before whom the case is

15 pending or to whom it is assigned is prejudiced against such party or

16 the interest of such party so that such party cannot or believes that

17 he cannot have a fair and impartial hearing before such Judge.

18 I declare under penalty of perjury that the foregoing is true and

19 correct.

20 Dated this 19th day of October, 1987 at anywhere, Callifornia.

21   John Doe
                            Defendant
22

AFFIDAVIT OF PREJUDICE

FIGURE 11

CHAPTER 15

ARREST AND RELEASE

A traffic ticket or citation, physical arrest at the scene, on an arrest or bench warrant or a "come in" letter telling you to come to court or face arrest are all means used by the law to get you into court.

If you have been involved in a accident you may not necessarily be arrested or given a citation. Sometime later, you may receive a "come in" letter notifying you that charges have been filed against you, that you have to appear in court on a specific date and that if you do not appear a warrant for your arrest will be issued.

If you appear in court on the date set, it is most likely that you will be allowed to remain at liberty and released on your own recognisance or "O.R.". If you don't show up, a warrant of arrest will be issued. These cases don't go away. I have seen people arrested and brought into court as much as ten years after issuance of the warrant. Although some jurisdictions will clear their warrant files on the less serious cases after five years.

The words "citation" and "traffic ticket" mean the same thing. A citation is an arrest and release without bail, on your "O.R.", on the spot. A failure to appear in court on the date set on the citation will result in a warrant for your arrest.

An arrest warrant may be obtained by the police from the court. Approval by the prosecuting attorney is usually required. If you are lucky some officer may call and tell you that a warrant has issued and to come to court as soon as possible. If you appear in court on your own you will probably be left at liberty on your "O.R.". However, you may be required to go to the police station to be booked: i.e.; fingerprinted, photographed and basic identification taken and then released.

Unfortunately, usually the police just come out and arrest you. You are taken to jail and booked. You may not get to court that day and certainly not if you are arrested on a holiday or weekend.

Once arrested and taken to the police station you have some important decisions to make.

•Do you answer questions other than name, address, age, birthdate or employment? Usually, the best answer is no. If the police have a case against you, they will not need your statements. If they do not have a case they can use your statements to try and make one. It is always a revelation to read a police report to someone and hear them say, "I didn't say that". It then becomes your word against that of the officer. Statements are rarely tape recorded or taken down in shorthand. Video taping is rarer though it does occur in some special cases such as driving under the influence.

•Do you want to bail out or take a chance on getting an "O.R." (without bail) release from the court?

You are entitled to a release on bail in all cases except for certain murder cases and violations of probation or parole. Since traffic cases don't usually involve such circumstances, you can bail out.

Bail is the posting of money or property (by deed) to ensure your appearance in court. Bail is usually set according to a bail schedule that has been approved by the courts for each individual crime. After you have been arrested you will, usually, be told how much bail will be required.

You may, if you or a relative have enough money, post a cash bail. The entire amount of cash bail, less a small processing fee, is refundable when the case is over, unless you or the person putting up the money authorize its use as a fine.

Some states may allow the posting of a percentage cash bail. For example; ten percent of the entire amount, with a promise to pay the rest if you fail to appear.

Otherwise you will have to post a Bail Bond through a bonding agency. Usually, these agencies are listed in the telephone book under "Bail Bonds" and there will probably be at least one such agency within sight of the jail. The bonding agency will post a bond guaranteeing your appearance in court. The bondsman will require a nonrefundable cash fee, usually ten percent of the total bail, plus require the signing over of certain security, like a house or car, before he will post the bond.

If you fail to appear, the bond is forfeited; that is, the court will require payment of the full amount of the bond by the bonding company. The bonding agency will take over the signed over property and may come looking for you. Bounty Hunters do exist. In addition, the people whose property was forfeited may be looking for you, because if you are brought in and surrendered to the court it is possible to have the forfeiture set aside, thus saving their property and money. This surrender to the court must take place within a certain period of time after the forfeiture, usually six months.

• **Who do you call and how?**

You are, usually, entitled to at least two telephone calls.   Keep them short.   The calls may not be free.   It is a very good idea to carry four dimes with you at all times.   Tape them to the back of your auto club card or other identification.   Call collect.   You may need those dimes later.   If you are not successful in contacting anyone who can help, you may have access to a telephone in the court lockup, so hang on to those dimes.   Your money is usually returned to you after booking so that you have it in jail.   DO NOT show that money in the lockup, you could be robbed.

The first person to call is your attorney. He can do more for you at this stage than anyone else.   This call is supposed to be confidential.   However, since the call is usually at a pay phone with police walking in and out you should be careful of what you say.   Your attorney can make arrangements for bail and has access to the police department, by law, where other individuals cannot get in to see you.   In fact, it is a crime, in most states to prevent or refuse to allow a attorney access to his client in jail.   It is a good idea to have the number of the attorney in your wallet, along with the dimes.

An attorney from the public defender's office is usually only allowed to come to the jail to advise you regarding your constitutional rights.   He can do nothing else before being appointed by the court to represent you.   He will not act to make bail arrangements or to contact family, arrange for witnesses, blood tests and so on.

You can call a family member or friend to ask them to call an attorney for you and make arrangements for bail.   Hope that they are reliable and will follow your instructions.   These calls may not be confidential and are probably monitored.   Be careful of what you say.   Most visiting booths have some form of monitoring.

You can call a bailbond agency directly. The bondsman will be happy to talk with you. How helpful they will be if you do not have enough cash for their fee up front will depend upon the agency. Remember the cash fee that you pay them is NOT refundable.

Remember that you will have to post bail for each warrant and in each jurisdiction. The bail can usually be posted at the main county jail. The local jail and/or court may not be willing or able to accept bail for other localities within the state. In such cases it may be easier for a bonding agency to put together a bail package than having your family or friends try to find out the location and amount of each warrant and go to each jail or courthouse to post bail.

•KEEP CALM! You may be treated with dignity and respect or with such callousness as to make you want to tear down the place. The best reaction is to keep calm. If you are unable to post bail within a "reasonable time" you will be booked, searched and locked up.

The search will probably be a "strip search". In such a search you literally strip naked while an officer examines you and searches your body cavities. A female is supposed to be searched by a female. California has enacted new laws which will, hopefully, diminish "strip searches" in the case of minor traffic arrests. This trend should be spread across the country. But the qualification on that limitation is that if the police officer suspects that drugs or weapons are involved he may perform such a total search. If such limitations are not in effect where and when you are arrested you will have to "grin and bear it".

If you decide to wait until court to see if you can get released without bail, good luck. Conditions will vary considerably. If you are in a local lockup things might not be too bad. If you find yourself heading for the main jail, it is suggested you reconsider and try to get out. If you are a woman, it is strongly urged that you should try to get bailed out, especially if you are to be taken to the main jail.

You should know that if arrested on a Friday, weekend or holiday you are not going to get to court until at least the following working day for the court. In addition, if the police are seeking a filing of charges against you more serious than a traffic warrant or ticket; they may take, in California, up to 48 hours for a misdemeanor and up to 72 hours for a felony. If they take longer than that they are supposed to bring you to court or release you. But if you are not released, you are not entitled to an automatic dismissal of your case. You have to show "prejudice"; that is, some reason that the delay has damaged your case. It is rare that the courts find such "prejudice" in your behalf.

Obviously, if you have warrants in other jurisdictions you will have to deal with them one court at a time, usually one day at a time. True, you may get "time served" by the time you finish your circuit. The judge will usually ask you how long you have been in custody and if it has been several days he may simply give you credit for that time in custody instead of any additional fine or time. Therefore, it may be worthwhile to tough it out.

If you plead not guilty your case will be set for trial. The judge will set bail or release you without bail. You may ask him to release you without bail, but he probably will not do so if you are brought in on a warrant for failure to appear or to pay a previous fine.

CHAPTER 16

PUNISHMENT

If you lose your trial or plead guilty or no contest (*nolo contendere*) you will be facing some form of punishment.

Most simple moving violations are only punishable by a fine. In most cases, where state law does provide for an alternate jail sentence, the court or prosecution will designate ahead of time (at the arraignment), that no jail is possible. The reason for this is to avoid having to appoint attorneys and provide jury trials in such cases.

In the usual traffic case all that happens when you are found guilty or plead guilty, is that the judge will tell you what the fine is and ask you if you need time to pay. If you have already posted bail he will decide how much of it to apply to the fine. They rarely go above the posted bail. You could also get a suspended sentence; that is, you are sentenced but do not have to do the sentence. In the other cases you will be faced with community service, probation, restitution, jail, alcohol or drug programs and license suspensions.

The judge may question you as to your driving record. Be honest. He probably will have a teletype in front of him showing your record, commonly called a "rap sheet". He is probably trying to get a feel for you and your attitude. If you don't remember, say so. Remember, after you have been convicted you have no right to remain silent. He may ask if you want to make a statement or you may ask to make a statement if you wish to be heard before he imposes sentence. This will give you an opportunity to try to convince him to either suspend the fine or give you less of a sentence than standard. He may give you a lecture. Be quiet and listen respectfully. Now is NOT the time to argue. If the judge tells you to stop talking, do so. Otherwise, you could be held in contempt. (See APPENDIX C—Contempt.)

If you don't have the money to pay a fine say so at the time of sentencing. The judge will most likely give you some form of charitable work to let you work off the fine. If you can not raise the money to pay the fine, bring what money you have and ask for an extension. If you have no money come to court anyway and explain. Ask to be allowed to do charitable work instead of the fine.

Otherwise payment is immediate and cash is preferred. Many courts will accept a good personal check or credit card. It is a good idea to ask the judge if such will be accepted before you leave the courtroom. If the clerk won't accept a check or credit card you will have to come back before the judge to ask for an extension of time to pay.

It is preferable to pay the fine in person and to be sure to get a receipt for the payment. One very common excuse heard is that "I gave the money to my wife, brother, sister, daughter, friend or other party to pay my fine." This explanation is not usually believed. It will not excuse you from having to pay again.

If you are paying by mail be exceptionally careful. Pay by money order made out to the clerk of the court with your name and case number on the money order. Make a photocopy of the money order. Then send it by registered mail, return receipt requested.

Keep all the receipts and the photocopy. They are your proof that you did indeed pay the fine in case it gets lost in the mail and a warrant is issued for your arrest.

> *This writer remembers getting a letter telling him that a warrant of arrest was being issued because he hadn't paid a ticket. It turned out that he had loaned his car to his girl friend and she had gotten the ticket. She was too embarrassed to tell him and mailed in the fine which got lost. Luckily she came by as he was reading the letter and the matter was cleared up.*

If, after a date has been set to pay a fine you find that you need more time, you should come to court and ask for another extension of time. This should be done before the due date of the fine, if possible. You do this by going to court and asking the traffic clerk for a extension of time to pay the fine. The clerk may be able to give you one extension without sending you into court. If you need more than one extension, however, it will probably be necessary for you to see the judge and ask him.

IMPORTANT! If you are not able to pay the fine or complete the charitable work before the date set COME TO COURT anyway and explain. The courts will usually work with you. If you do not come to court you will probably end up in jail. Do not try to get out of any penalty. The judge may treat that as contempt and jail you. In most cases if you have been trying to comply the court will work with you. He will give you more time, convert the fine into community service or possibly, if you have had particularly bad circumstances, the fine may be suspended. But

COME TO COURT.

You cannot be jailed for failing to pay a fine if you tried but were financially unable to do so. However, if it appears that you have merely neglected to pay or made no effort to do so then you are really facing jail time. At the very least, therefore, make some sort of payment or come to court before the fine is due and tell the judge that you are unable to pay and request community service. Be sure to do the community service that is assigned. If you fail to do so you will be looking at a jail sentence.

If you do not show up, a warrant will be issued for your arrest and the department of motor vehicles will probably be notified so that your privilege to drive will be suspended.

It is vital to remember that the courts will work with you if you are trying to comply with the court orders and can show that you are so doing. The scofflaw is the one who ends up in jail.

If you are convicted of a more serious driving violation, then you may be put under the supervision of the court for a period of time while you are required to comply with certain conditions of the court. This is called probation.

The judge may continue your sentencing for a period of time in order to have a report on you prepared. This is called a "Probation Report". This is usually done in the more serious misdemeanors and all felonies so that he can look at your background and record more thoroughly before deciding on a sentence. These reports usually take three to four weeks. The judge can, however, put you on probation without getting a report.

This probation may be unsupervised, commonly called "summary probation" or a "conditional release in the community". What this means is that if you fail to comply with the terms of the probation and/or commit another violation of the law and the court finds out about it you can be brought back into court and sentenced to the maximum available sentence for the original crime as well as be sentenced for any other crime which you may have committed.

The other type of probation is supervised or "formal" probation. This means that you will be under the supervision of a probation officer to whom you will have to report on a regular basis. This type of probation is used when the court wants to be sure that you are complying with its conditions; such as drug and alcohol programs, drug testing or simply to keep an eye on you if you have a bad record. If the probation officer feels that you have violated any of the terms and conditions of probation he will schedule a court hearing to bring the matter to the attention of the judge.

In these days of expanding use of computers it is becoming easier to keep track of new violations. If it appears that you are on probation in some district in the state and are convicted of a new crime, it is possible that the original court will be contacted and you will eventually be notified to come to that court to face a hearing on whether you are in violation of that probation. On the other hand, it can be astonishing how much is not entered into or picked up by the computer systems.

License suspensions may be imposed by both the judge and the department of motor vehicles for a variety of reasons.

•If you have gotten too high a point count the DMV will suspend your license or rather your privilege to drive. You can also be put on some type of driving probation or restriction.

•If you are convicted of an alcohol or drug related offense or one involving dangerous or reckless conduct the judge may be able to suspend your driving privilege immediately upon sentencing. In some cases, if you need to drive to work, your license may be limited for such purpose only.

•If you refuse to take a blood alcohol test after a proper arrest.

Your car may be impounded in the case of some drug and alcohol offenses for a certain period of time unless you can convince the judge otherwise. This can be quite expensive as most impound yards will charge about $25 to $30 per day all of which you will have to pay to get your car out of impound.

Jail is being imposed more and more. Normally a jail sentence will be imposed only when your conduct has been much too serious for the court to consider other alternatives. The jail sentence may also be given in combination with other penalties such as fines and probation conditions. Our legislators are enacting mandatory jail sentences thus taking any discretion out of the hands of the judges.

The amount of jail time will vary depending upon the offense. If you are working or going to school, it may be possible to request that you do your time on weekends. In many states where conditions in the jails are extremely overcrowded the jailers will try to shorten the actual time you do, usually pursuant to authorizing legislation or court order. This is done by giving time off for good behavior, for working in the jail or being available and willing to work if there is no work available. Work release programs are also used, such as working for the department of highways.

You usually have a right to be sentenced right away or you can request that the sentencing may be postponed. In California, for instance, you have a right to have the judge wait six hours before imposing sentence. This may not be a bad idea as it may give the judge a chance to cool down if he is mad at you.

> *This writer remembers one judge who gave very hard sentences in the morning but if you could continue the sentencing until after lunch you could usually get a lighter sentence as he was in a much more mellow mood.*

The judge must sentence you, usually, within five days after the finding of guilty or you will be entitled to a new trial. However, you must ask for the new trial before you are sentenced. If you do not object you lose this right.

You can also request a stay of execution; that is, for a period of time to go by before you have to start serving your sentence. A stay can be important because you may need time to get your affairs in order. For example; if your license is going to be suspended and you have driven to court, a stay will allow you to drive home legally.

Administrative penalties may be imposed by the state in addition to the sentence by the judge. These penalties will probably take the form of a license restriction, suspension, or revocation. (See Chapter 17—Licensing.)

As mentioned before, in the usual traffic case all that happens when you are found guilty or plead guilty is that the judge will tell you what the fine is and ask you if you need time to pay. If you have already posted bail he will decided how much of it to apply to the fine. The judge will rarely go above the posted bail.

If you feel that the sentence of the judge was unfair or illegal you do have the right to appeal from that sentence. (See APPENDIX D—Appeals.)

CHAPTER 17

LICENSING

Driving is considered by all states to be a privilege not a right. *You must be licensed in order to drive a motor vehicle upon a public highway.* Therefore when you apply for a license and are granted one it is a privilege which is controlled by the state. This privilege can be suspended or revoked; that is, temporarily or permanently taken away. You can be placed on administrative probation which can limit the scope of your license and which if violated by another traffic violation or violation of the terms of the probation will result in the temporary or permanent loss of the license or privilege to drive. There can also be criminal penalties.

For the sake of convenience, the various licensing agencies of the states will be referred to as the Department of Motor Vehicles and abbreviated as "DMV". In addition, when reference is made to suspension or revocation of a driver's license, this means that the privilege to drive is what is affected.

•In obtaining your license all states require an examination which will demonstrate your ability to drive properly and your knowledge of the rules of the road and the applicable law.

This information is contained in a licensing manual obtainable from the DMV. The licensing manual will also explain the various ways in which you can lose your privilege to drive. If you pass the test they will issue a temporary license which is valid for a certain number of days. A permanent license will be sent after all your papers are processed and a records check is made to see if you are entitled to a permanent license.

In some cases, showing your license to the traffic clerk or the judge may get a no license charge dismissed or the fine reduced or suspended.

The judge will usually want to see a permanent license. Therefore, simply ask to continue the arraignment of your case until you have received the permanent license. You do this by giving up your right to a speedy trial. It may take from sixty to one hundred and twenty days to obtain a hard copy of your license if the DMV is busy. Most courts will agree to such a lengthy continuance when you tell them the reason.

•If your privilege to drive has been revoked or suspended you may still be able to get the privilege reinstated, if the time of the suspension or revocation has elapsed. Such reinstatement does NOT automatically occur by the lapse of time. You must apply to the Department of Motor Vehicles for reinstatement. There is usually a records check and a special fee. Therefore, when you apply for reinstatement of your driving privilege, be sure to notify the clerk that you are applying for "reinstatement". This word has specific meaning to the DMV clerks. They will run a special records check and be able to tell you what steps you have to take to get your driving privilege back.

Be careful in filling out your license application. Be honest. You sign most of those applications under "penalty of perjury" or actually swear a oath before a clerk that what is in the application is true and correct. If you lie, you have committed "PERJURY", a felony. They do prosecute such offenses.

Your driving privilege can be suspended or revoked for several reasons:

•Not reporting your involvement in a traffic accident. Most states require that when you have been involved in a traffic accident where there has been damage over a certain amount ($250 for example) or if there has been an injury or death, you must report it to the DMV, usually within a fairly short time limit. If you fail to do so, then your license can be suspended.

•Failure to pay a civil judgment: If you are sued because of an traffic accident and lose and thereafter you fail to pay the civil judgment which has been obtained against you, your license may be suspended for a period of time until you have paid the judgement and can show proof of insurance. It is very important to be sure that such judgements are paid. It is especially important when you are being represented by an insurance company. It is not uncommon for the company to fail to notify the state department of motor vehicles that the judgement has been paid with the result being that your license is suspended.

•Being involved in too many accidents in a one year period.

•A conviction of Driving While Under the Influence of Alcohol and/or Drugs. Such a conviction carries with it possible suspension by the judge. Two or more convictions will result in up to five years of suspension or revocation by either the court or the "DMV", or both. A juvenile in California, for example, will upon conviction lose his license until he is 18 or for one year whichever occurs first.

•A conviction of vehicular manslaughter usually has at least a one year mandatory revocation.

•Too many moving violation "points" may cause the DMV to find you to be a "Negligent Driver". This means that each type of moving violation is given a numeric value. If you add up too many points over a one, two or three year period the DMV will declare you a negligent driver. You may be put on probation instead of immediately losing your license and required to go to a driver education class and have no further violations. Any other moving violations will result in instant loss of license.

For example, in California each simple moving violation is given a value of one point. A more serious violation as DUI, hit and run, speed contest or reckless driving will have a value of two points. Thereafter, if you get four points in one year, six points in two or eight points in three your license will be suspended.

•Refusal to take and/or complete a blood, breath or urine test after an arrest for DUI will result in a suspension or revocation after sentence. In some states, the police officer is empowered to take your license immediately upon your refusal and turn it into the court as well as schedule a suspension the court within a few days. This is before any finding of guilt.

•Letting someone else use your license or your violation of some restriction which has been placed on your license will result in suspension.

•A conviction of some type of drug offense or other crime specified by statute involving the use of your car can also result in suspension.

Notice of suspension or revocation will be given to you either directly—by the judge, hearing officers, DMV personnel or police officer—or indirectly by mail.

The notice will usually tell you the reason for the suspension, when it takes effect and the duration. *You may have a right to a hearing to contest the proposed suspension.* You will be notified in the letter of suspension if you have such a right. If you fail to request the hearing as instructed in the notice the revocation/suspension will take place as specified. You will also be told what steps you will need to take to have your privilege reinstated when the suspension period is over. Read the letter carefully. Save it.

If you request the hearing as directed, the suspension will be not take effect until after the hearing has been held and you have lost.

The DMV hearing can be either formal or informal. A formal hearing will have the proceedings reported in some manner such as a court reporter or a tape recording and will have the reasons for the decision written up. This can be valuable if you intend to fight an adverse decision in a court of law. However, your chances of success are slight and you may prefer a informal hearing. You must check with each board to find out what is actually involved in each state.

At the hearing, the reasons for your proposed suspension will be presented. If the reason was for a refusal to take a chemical test, then the officer will be present to establish the necessary elements; namely, a lawful arrest, the fact that he properly informed you of the requirement of a test and the tests available and that your license would be suspended if you refused and how you refused.

You may be represented by an attorney at such a hearing although you will not be entitled to appointed counsel if you are indigent. Of course, you may represent yourself. In any event, remember the same factors of preparation and appearance as mentioned before for trial. The hearing officer will be watching you all the time, so dress appropriately and act appropriately. Be polite. Be concise. Do not get outraged no matter what you hear. As mentioned before, you are being judged even before you testify.

You may present witnesses to show why the proposed suspension shouldn't take place. For example; character witnesses as to good driving, your employer as to his need for you to be able to drive, etc.. Your attitude is extremely critical at these hearings. If you come across as the outraged citizen you will probably lose. A contrite attitude is best. In the case of a refusal to take a chemical test after a DUI arrest, it will be your word against that of the officer if you maintain that you really did not refuse or that the test(s) were never offered to you. You cannot claim inability to complete a test as a defense or that you wanted to consult with your attorney before making up your mind if you should take a test or which one to take. Further, it does not help if you were not told of the other available tests but only that one type (usually breath) was available.

If you convince the hearing officer in your favor, you may not get any suspension or you may be placed on probation. If he is not impressed, you will lose your license.

You may have the right to appeal the decision of the hearing officer by having your case referred to a court of law. These procedures vary considerably from state to state and change rapidly. Therefore, if the ruling is made against you and you wish to appeal, ask the hearing officer if the ruling is appealable. He probably will not tell you how to go about the appeal and it will be up to you to check the local rules. It is rare for the rulings in these administrative hearings to be overturned.

Many of these hearings, especially the formal type, will be recorded in some way. You can obtain a copy or transcript of the proceedings and this may be useful if your case goes to trial.

If you continue to drive after your license has been suspended or revoked you are committing a crime. In addition, if you have previously been convicted of such a crime you will be facing increased penalties.

Thirty states have signed a Driver License Compact. This Compact provides that if one of the member states has suspended or revoked your license then it will be considered suspended or revoked in each of the other member states. In other words, if you try to get a license or drive in any of the member states while your driving privilege is suspended or revoked in another member state you will be committing a crime.The member states as of May 1985 are: Alabama, Arizona, Arkansas, California, Colorado, Delaware, Florida, Hawaii, Idaho, Illinois, Indiana, Iowa, Kansas, Louisiana, Maine, Mississippi, Montana, Nebraska, Nevada, New Jersey, New Mexico, New York, Oklahoma, Oregon, Tennessee, Utah, Vermont, Virginia, Washington, and West Virginia.

The crime of Driving with a Suspended or Revoked Privilege to Drive requires that you be driving a motor vehicle upon a highway with the knowledge that your privilege to drive has been suspended, restricted or revoked. It is not required that you have a driver's license for this crime to be committed.

The important element here is that you have knowledge of the suspension or revocation. If you, in fact, have not received notice you are not guilty of the crime. The most commonly used method of notice of suspension is by mail. There is a presumption that if the notice has been properly mailed you have received it. However, this is hard to prove unless there is a signed return receipt.

So, if the means of notifying you of the suspension or revocation was by mail, you can sometimes negotiate a suspended license charge into a lesser charge of driving with no valid license. This is important because in California as well as other states the crime of driving with a suspended or revoked license carries with it a mandatory jail sentence and is usable as a prior conviction. That is a conviction that can be used to increase penalties if you get arrested more than once for the same offense and this usually means mandatory jail.

If you did not actually receive notice and the prosecution will not reduce the charge then go to trial. The defense procedure is the same as for any other crime. If you have moved before the notice was sent to your old address, be prepared to show proof of some kind of the date of your move. While you are usually required to notify the DMV of any move, failure to do so will not prevent you from using the defense of having moved.

If you have not moved but did not receive the notice, just testify that way and argue about the reliability of the U.S. Postal Service.

CHAPTER 18

MOTIONS

Motions are requests by either party to the law suit to have something done by the court. *There are many such motions: motions for continuances, motions to suppress evidence, motions to dismiss for lack of speedy trial, motions to dismiss for lack of speedy arraignment, motions to have the case transferred to the county seat, motions to have the judge disqualified, motions to change attorney, motions to have a court reporter and so on.* As you can see there are many motions that can be made.

Most of the above motions should be made before trial. They can be made at the time of arraignment, especially motions to dismiss for lack of speedy arraignment and motions to transfer to the county seat.

•A Refusal to Stipulate or agree to have a commissioner or hearing officer decide your case is not a motion to disqualify. Instead, when you are asked to agree or stipulate, you simply state that you wish to have a judge hear your case. You are entitled to have a judge decide your case so your request must be granted. Thereafter, when your case is assigned to a judge, you may then move to disqualify him if you do not like him.

•Motions to disqualify the judge must be made before trial and must be made a specific time before the actual trial date if you know in advance who the actual trial judge is going to be. This time period is usually ten days before the date of the trial. If you don't know which judge will be hearing your case you don't have to make your motion until you find out the name of the assigned judge.

There are usually two different ways to disqualify a judge. The first is where you simply state that he is prejudiced against you without having to state a reason. This is called an "Affidavit of Prejudice". Usually, these motions must be granted, if made "timely"; that is, within the proper time limits. You are, however, limited to one of these challenges per case. The other motion to disqualify is called an "Affidavit for Cause"; that is, you must make a motion specifying the actual reasons for requesting that judge not hear your case. These motions are unlimited in number but in practice are rarely used and rarely granted. Of course, if you can show that the judge indicated that there was no possible way he would believe you or your witnesses and did so in front of witnesses you can be sure that there would be no trouble getting the motion granted. In traffic court there is usually not much fuss made in granting these motions if there are enough judges available. If you are in a one or two judge court it is an entirely different matter. (See Figure 11 for a sample form.)

You should be aware that judges have usually made arrangements for hearing officers because they are too busy with what they consider more important matters. There is always the likelihood that you might be regarded with disfavor. However, if you get the feeling that you can not get a fair trial do not hesitate to disqualify. Remember, you should have already been to court to watch the judicial officers in action so you have some idea of what they are like and if you are willing to have them hear your case.

This type of motion is made without any need for notifying the prosecution.

•A motion to dismiss for lack of speedy trial may be made orally if you have not given up your right to a speedy trial or "waived time" and object if the court tries to continue the case beyond the specified time limit. This is usually forty-five days from the time of arraignment if not in custody at that time or thirty if you were in custody when arraigned for traffic and misdemeanors.

•A motion for a continuance will usually be heard orally and granted if you have notified the prosecution ahead of time that you will be requesting such a continuance, so that witnesses can be called off. If you wait until the day of trial and witnesses are present you will probably be out of luck. However, many rules of court require such a request be in writing, and you should try to find this out ahead of time from the clerk of the court. The rules requiring written motions to continue are not often followed except in federal court. But to be absolutely safe you cannot go wrong by filing a written motion.

All other motions are governed by specific formalities. In many cases, especially in traffic court, these formalities may be given up or "waived" by the court and the prosecution. However, if you are intending to appeal a loss then you should follow the formalities. The rules for such motions are usually contained in a book called "Rules of Court". (See APPENDIX A—Law Books.)

There must be a "Notice of Motion" and a "Motion". *They must both be in writing and the prosecution and the court must be given advance notice of the motion, unless waived (given up) by the prosecution and the court.* Ten days before the hearing is a standard time limit. That is, you must serve the notice of motion and the motion by giving a copy of the papers of the notice and motion to the prosecution and the court at least ten days before the date scheduled for hearing. The original goes to the court clerk for filing in the court file and is for the judge and you keep a copy.

There are usually four parts to a motion:

•Notice of Motion. This notifies the court and the prosecution that you intend to make a specific motion on a specific date and time.

•The Motion. This contains the matter which you are requesting. This will be attached to the Notice of Motion.

•Points and Authorities commonly referred to as "P&A's". This consists of a listing of the legal basis for your motion with the court cases which support your position and is attached to and follows the motion itself.

•Proof of Service. This is a statement, usually the last page of the documents, that you have had served a copy of all the moving papers on the prosecution, either personally by a person other than yourself or by mail to the address of the prosecution. (See Figure 14.)

Most motions are typed on numbered double spaced 8 1/2" x 11" paper. Some courts require that legal paper of either 8 1/2" by 13" or 14" be used. However, even handwritten motions will be accepted. They should be readable of course and the lines numbered.

The other mentioned motions require specific form and formalities in addition to a quoting ("citing") of the appropriate law. Since changes in the law occur so rapidly we are not going to attempt to cover the matter here. It is recommended that you check with your local law library and look into a form file which you may be able to follow. (Be sure it is recent.) It is recommended that you consider hiring an attorney or paralegal to assist you in the preparation of such papers.

•Motions to Suppress Evidence are based on the Constitution of the United States Article IV—the right to be secure from unreasonable search and seizure. Most states have also adopted this right into their state constitutions. This type of motion may also be based upon appropriate state law. Such a motion is rare in the usual traffic case where the officer states that he has seen a violation and you dispute that observation.

However, if you or your car are searched and something illegal is found, or observed (such as your drunken condition or the results of a chemical test) this becomes a very important motion. Again, the law changes drastically from month to month and from state to state. If you feel that this is an issue in your case, it is again recommended that you consult with an attorney, at least for some guidance.

Name, address and telephone no. of attorney(s)

This space for court clerk only

Attorney(s) for

| DECLARATION FOR SUBPOENA DUCES TECUM | IN THE MUNICIPAL COURT OF .... JUDICIAL DISTRICT COUNTY OF .... STATE OF CALIFORNIA .... | Case Number |

.... vs. ....
Plaintiff(s)   Defendant(s)

I, the undersigned, say: I am the .... in the above-entitled action;

said action has been set for ....

on .... at .... M., in Division ....

.... of the above-named court; that ....

.... (name of person)

has in his possession or under his control the following: (Designate and name the exact thing(s) to be produced)

The above is material to the issues involved in this case by reason of the following facts:

Executed on .... at Los Angeles County California.
                          (date)

I declare under penalty of perjury that the foregoing is true and correct.

....
Declarant

NOTE: COPY OF THIS DECLARATION MUST BE SERVED WITH A COPY OF THE SUBPOENA DUCES TECUM.

DECLARATION FOR SUBPOENA DUCES TECUM

76D176K— **Ci29**—(1) PS 2-84   C.C.P. 1985-1987.5, 2015.5, P.C. 1326

DECLARATION
SUBPOENA DUCES TECUM

FIGURE 12

CHAPTER 19

JUVENILE COURT

In most states juveniles are treated differently from adults. The proceedings are considered "civil" in nature and thus juveniles are not entitled, except by statute, to jury trials. Convictions of crimes were not, until recently, considered as criminal convictions and were not usable in adult court. *However, most departments of licensing and/or motor vehicles were and are entitled to use juvenile traffic convictions to limit, suspend or revoke a juvenile's privilege to drive.*

The terminology of juvenile court may be confusing at first, and varies from state to state. It may be completely different from that used in adult court. In California, for example, the juvenile is often referred to as the "minor". The charges against him are contained in a "petition" which is brought on his "behalf". The trial is referred to as an "adjudication". Instead of being found guilty, the petition is found to be "true" and "sustained". Not guilty is termed "not true" and the petition is "dismissed". Sentencing is referred to as a "disposition". In addition, the juvenile's name is not released to the public. If the case is appealed, the juvenile is referred to by his first name and middle initial such as "In re (in the case of) Gladys R.". The juvenile may be fined, given community service to do, be placed on probation and/or jailed in juvenile hall. If the crime for which he is convicted is not one in which jail could be imposed for an adult then the juvenile cannot be locked up, at first.

However, if he does not comply with his conditions of probation, if placed on probation, he can then be locked up.

•In most states when a juvenile gets a traffic ticket he is given a citation and he and one or both of his parents or legal guardians must appear with him at the juvenile hearing.

•Juvenile moving violations, except for driving under the influence, hit and run and reckless driving, are usually held in front of a "hearing officer"in the larger jurisdictions. He is not an elected judge but a person appointed by the judges to hear cases. The minor will be informed that he has a right to have his case heard by a judge and asked to give up that right. It is usually safe to do so.

One of the hazards of asking that the case be handled by a judge is that it will then be entered into the regular juvenile proceedings. This means that upon a conviction, instead of fairly informal treatment, the minor will usually end up on formal probation under the supervision of a probation officer. It is worth while to avoid this if possible. Obviously, the more serious violations as mentioned previously will go directly into the regular juvenile court system.

•In other matters things will proceed in a similar manner to a regular court trial. Juveniles, except in a minority of the states, are not entitled to a jury trial. However, all other law applicable to adults will apply, including the right to counsel. As most juveniles are not employed and are therefore indigent, they are entitled to the public defender or other appointed counsel.

•The trend is for juveniles to be treated more and more as adults. In the more serious cases, juveniles may be found not fit for the juvenile courts and have their cases transferred to the adult courts and thereafter be treated the same as adults.

If you request a hearing at your arraignment, which is the equivalent of a trial, you will be given another court date when the officer will be present. Usually the prosecuting attorney will not be present and the hearing officer may conduct the questioning.

•Once a minor becomes an adult he can usually have his record sealed. This means that upon request, the court will enter an order closing his record and he can thereafter state he was never arrested. However, most states still allow the motor vehicle departments to use juvenile convictions along with the adult record for licensing matters.

•You should treat juvenile traffic matters as seriously as adult ones, even more so, because the effect of such violations can not only prevent actual licensing or cause cancellation of licenses, but may result in outrageous insurance premiums, or cancellation of your policy. For example, in California a conviction for DUI will result in a suspension of the juvenile's license for one year or until she is 18 whichever comes first and she must attend an alcohol program.

•Remember that in most states parents are responsible for the damages caused by their youngsters. For example, in Arizona, the parents or guardians are required to sign a "Legal Guardian Affidavit" which in effect makes them fully responsible for any damages caused by any "negligence or willful misconduct of a minor...when driving a motor vehicle upon a highway..."(Arizona Driver License Manual). If there has been a traffic accident, it is important to consult with an attorney to decide what to do. The rules are still the same as in adult court in this regard. In addition, the parents may be responsible for the costs of appointed counsel, costs of court, probation and lodging in a juvenile hall. Also, parents in states like California will be held responsible for the costs of Alcoholic and Drug Rehabilitation programs if their youngster is convicted of driving under the influence. Juvenile matters are not something to be taken lightly.

Therefore, fight it, if you can.

APPENDIX A

LAW BOOKS:
HOW TO FIND AND USE THEM

The sections of law governing moving violations may be found in different parts of the law books of the various states and municipalities.

Many states have most of the laws governing traffic violations collected in a book called the "Vehicle Code". This book, in paperback, may be available from the state Department of Motor Vehicles. If not available then you will have to check the sources mentioned below. The Driver Handbooks put out by each state will also contain, in abbreviated form and without the section numbers, most of the laws governing traffic violations. These books are available from the licensing departments of each state, either free or for a low fee.

In those states where the violations are part of the "Penal Code", you will probably have to look up the appropriate sections in a law library. Be sure you are getting an up to date edition.

Other states may have the laws listed under different names. For example, Federal criminal law is found in 7 U.S.C., that is the 7th. volume of the United States Codes as well as in other sections. These laws would be important if you were arrested in Washington, D.C., a Federal Park or on a Military Base. Names of law books containing the traffic laws of different states are, for example; "The Maryland Transportation Code", "The Kentucky Revised Statutes", "The New York Vehicle and Traffic Law", etc..

The law governing your violation may be found in varying places depending on the violation and, of course, the state.

The most important starting point is your traffic ticket. The officer will write down on your ticket the name and number of the violation and the name of the law book in which it can be found. For example: Violation 21802a V.C. would tell you the paragraph number and the book. Here, "V.C." would stand for the Vehicle Code. The officer will, usually, write a summary of the violation. The previous number would be translated as vehicle at posted stop sign failure to yield on right of way. "P.C." would mean the Penal Code. You should ask the officer what the initials mean. In any event, they are explained in the books themselves.

Some states, such as California, have these books for sale at the local department of motor vehicles at a reasonable sum and of course legal book stores. In other states, they may be purchased at legal book stores (usually they are very expensive). In all states, they are available to the public at the law library and might be found at your local library.

At the law library, you may get assistance in locating the specific section of the law and will be allowed to make a copy of it by the law librarian. The assistance you will be given will be limited to finding the appropriate books; they are not allowed to give legal advice.

You may locate the phone number and address of the law library in your telephone book, usually under the heading of the county government services. Otherwise call information, ask a lawyer, or ask at the courthouse.

Most courthouses will have a law library.   If you ask, you can make or pay to have made, a copy of the code section in which your are interested.   The librarian or clerk will probably do it for you if there are no other facilities available to the public.

The public libraries will, in addition to some law books, also contain books of general information covering various aspects of the law, such as this one. Look in the card catalogs under "law" to get referrals to other areas of interest. .

Be sure that you are getting the latest issue, as the laws can change often. Check inside the front cover to find out what year the book was issued. If your case is older than the current year, look for the book from the year in which the offense occurred. The law may be different. In most cases, the front of the book will identify what dates it is to cover or what year in which it is to be used.

There are two types of law books, annotated and unannotated. *This simply means that the annotated books have notes from all cases that have been appealed involving that specific section of the law.* These books are usually hard cover and are updated with "pocket parts". The unannotated books only contain a statement of the law without any cases mentioned. These are either hardcover or softcover. They are revised and reprinted each year.

•To use an unannotated law book you simply check the front of the book to be sure it is up to date. Then look up the number of the section. Be very careful of the numbering system as it must be exact. In addition, many of these volumes will contain sections from other law books. So be careful that you look up the right section.

•To use an annotated law book check the "pocket part" first to be sure it is up to date. Look at the cover of the paper "pocket part". There will be information telling what year is covered. The pocket part is usually found at the back of the book. Check there for the code section first. If it is not in the pocket part then look in the hardcover book. Look at the front page. There will be information telling what year is covered.

Following the statement of the law will be a list of cases with explanations of what a court held them to mean in regards to a violation of that section. Read them to see if one or more applies to your situation. Then go into the main book and do the same. These annotations are abbreviations of the case. Once you have read them and feel that one or more is useful you then use the citation given to locate the law book with the actual case. Then read that case. If you feel that it still applies to you then you can tell the judge what you have found. If you do this the judge may well ask you for the "cite" or "citation" so that he can look up the case to see what it says. This means the name and number of the case. For example: 128 C.A.3rd. 356 (1978) would mean volume number 128 of the California Appellate Reports, Third Edition, page 356 in year 1978.

"Rules of Court" are books which contain the procedures used by the various courts in the state. They will give you detailed information as to the times for filing certain motions or appeals and the forms which are to be used. These books are in every law library as well as the courthouse.

If your needs of research become more detailed then you should consider consulting an attorney or paralegal. He will have the books available and know how to use them.

APPENDIX B

USE OF A SUBPOENA

You will need to use a court order called a "subpoena" if you must have a witness or item of evidence brought to court at a specific time.

There are two types of subpoenas. The first and most commonly used is a order for a witness to appear and is simply called a *"Subpoena"*. The second is called a *"Subpoena Dueces Tecum"* or *"SDT"* and is for the production of a physical item of evidence such as a document. The major difference between the two subpoenas is that in a SDT you must file a "declaration" stating that the requested item is necessary for your case. (See Figures 3 and 12.)

•In order to issue a subpoena you must get the appropriate form(s) from the clerk's office of the court. Fill it out carefully. You fill in the name of the case, the case number, the time, date, court room, and place. You then have the clerk stamp it and have it served upon the desired person. In the case of a "SDT" fill out and file the "declaration". The subpoena listing the requested item is served on the person who would be the legal custodian of the item. The subpoena would be normally addressed to the "Custodian of Records". That person would be required to bring or send the subpoenaed item to court. Subpoenas in criminal cases including traffic are free. However, serving the subpoena may cost.

• In order for a subpoena to be valid it must be personally served and have proof of service filed with the court.

Valid service requires that the original subpoena be shown to the person being served and a copy of the subpoena given to her by the server of the subpoena.   The server of the subpoena, sometimes called a process server, must then sign the subpoena, usually on the back.   He ceritifies "under penalty of perjury" that he is an adult, not a party to the action and that he served the subpoena on the named person at a particular time, date and location.

•The process server must be someone who is not a party to the action and who is an adult.   In other words, neither you as defendant nor one of your other witnesses can serve the subpoena.   You may use a law enforcement agency such as a marshal's or sheriff's office, a professional process server, or a nonprofessional third party to serve the subpoena.

The difference between servers is cost, speed, efficiency and ability.   Law enforcement agencies usually need at least ten days in which they will try to serve the subpoena and will only try a few times to serve it—unless they are acting for the prosecution.   A professional process server as well as a third party can probably serve the subpoena very rapidly and more persistently.   Obviously, the price charged will reflect the type of service given.   You should check with each to find out their requirements as to time and cost.   If you are using a friend, there may be no cost but he may have difficulty in serving the subpoena which a professional would not have. Process serving can sometimes be dangerous.

•The subpoena and proof of service will be returned to the person requesting the subpoena.   There is also a place to indicate if the person subpoenaed could not be served.

•You will need to file such "proof of service"

with the court in order to show it to the judge only if the person subpoenaed does not appear in court or bring the subpoenaed item. The reason for this is that the judge must be sure that the person failing to appear has really been served before he makes a order for that person's arrest. That is why service is made by a person who is not a party to the trial.

•Failure to obey a subpoena is contempt of court and can result in arrest and imprisonment. In addition, if the person subpoenaed does not appear you can request and obtain a continuance of your case, for a reasonable time, until he does appear or is brought into court under arrest.

Obviously, in most cases, your witnesses are your friends and will come into court voluntarily. They may need the subpoena to get off of work. If they don't appear you need not tell the court or request a warrant for their arrest as you would for a hostile witness.

1	
2	John Doe
	700 Main Street
3	Anywhere, CA 900XX
	(712) 89`1-55ZZ
4	In Propria Persona

```
 1
 2   John Doe
     700 Main Street
 3   Anywhere, CA 900XX
     (712) 89`1-55ZZ
 4   In Propria Persona

 5

 6      MUNICIPAL COURT OF THE ANYWHERE JUDICAL DISTRICT
            COUNTY OF LOS ANGELES, STATE OF CALIFORNIA
 7

 8   PEOPLE OF THE STATE OF CALIFORNIA )
                             Plaintiff,)    Case #M684930
 9                                     )    Notice of Appeal
                                       )
10              vs.                    )
                                       )
11          JOHN DOE                   )
                         Defendant.)
12   ──────────────────────────────

13          Defendant, John Doe, hereby appeals from theverdict of

14   guilty and the sentence imposed upon him on October 5, 1987.

15

16      Dated this 19th. day of October, l987 at anywhere, Callifornia.

17                                    John Doe
                                      Defendant
18

19

20

21

22
```

NOTICE OF APPEAL

FIGURE 13

APPENDIX C

CONTEMPT OF COURT

This section is not intended to scare you or prevent you from fighting your ticket. Rather contempt of court is mentioned here so you won't be afraid to appear and talk in court. You will have the knowledge of how to avoid "Contempt".

"Contempt of Court" is when you have managed to get the judge mad at you. If he is mad because you have called him a name or demonstrated by some act your disregard of him, he can then hold you in contempt. If he is angry because of your actions before the case came to court, such as when you got the ticket, or because he has to find you not guilty, then you are not in contempt of court.

There are two types of contempt. "Direct Contempt" which occurs when the act or statement is done in front of the judge while within the courthouse. "Indirect Contempt" which occurs when the act or statements are made within the courthouse and told to the judge.

This effectively means that "Direct Contempt" can be punished immediately. A fine is usually imposed but if the judge is mad enough he could put you in jail. He could also give both a fine and jail. Where there is "Indirect Contempt", you are entitled to a hearing before another judge. In both cases, you are entitled to be represented by a lawyer.

If accused of contempt, APOLOGIZE. In most cases such apology will be accepted. You may get quite a bawling out but take it and keep your mouth shut. If your apology is not accepted then you will pay your fine or do your time, if you are in fact held in contempt.

You can fight the order of the judge holding you in contempt by running a "Writ of Habeas Corpus." You do this by requesting a stay of execution of your sentence from the judge so that you can run the Writ. Then, if the stay is granted, consult a lawyer immediately. These writs usually have to be done in a particular manner to be considered. If you decide to go it alone, consult your local law library immediately for the "Rules of Court" which will tell you what the higher court expects in such writ. There may also be a book of forms which will give a sample of such a writ which can be used. The Court of Appeals are usually more forgiving of lack of exactness when the writs are prepared by those who are not attorneys.

Examples of Direct Contempt are:
- You call the judge a SOB or similar.
- You use profanity in the courtroom.
- You refuse to shut up when the judge has told you to be quiet.
- You slam your hand or shoe or papers down on the counsel table in disgust.
- You stomp out of the courtroom, slamming the doors behind you.
- Your friends tell you loudly that you were robbed and you loudly agree.

You get the picture?

Examples of Indirect Contempt are:
- All of the above done while still in the courthouse and relayed back to the judge.
- Failure to obey a court order: such as not paying your fine or doing your community service.

Examples of No Contempt:

•When you do all of the above outside of the courthouse.

•It is not contempt of court but rather Contempt of Cop when you testify that you called the officer a SOB or other name when you got the ticket or said "Like Hell I did", in response to the officer's questioning, and may be why he wrote you up in the first place instead of giving you a warning.

As you can see from the above, the best advice you can be given is that if you get mad or outraged about what happens in court KEEP QUIET about it until you get out of the courthouse. Freedom of speech and action is limited in these particular circumstances.

In addition to the types of contempt discussed above, there is the crime of Contempt. This crime is usually a misdemeanor. It is charged in the same manner as any other misdemeanor and you are entitled to the same Constitutional rights as any other crime. This crime consists of violating a court order. Such orders are usually in the form of injunctions or restraining orders. The civil court could utilize its own contempt order by issuing what is called an "Order to Show Cause, In Re Contempt" which would require you to appear in front of the court to show why you should not be held in contempt. However, civil penalties are not very severe and in certain cases, a criminal charge of contempt could be filed. This would bring into play the longer jail sentences and heavier fines of the criminal court.

It would be highly unusual for such a criminal contempt charge to ever occur in any type of traffic offense whether they are infractions, misdemeanors or felonies. This information is presented so that if you should find yourself with such a charge of criminal contempt you can defend yourself. You would use the same techniques you would in fighting any other misdemeanor or felony. Again, the consultation and use of an attorney is highly recommended.

APPENDIX D

APPEALS

If you lose your case, you may want to appeal it. This procedure is very complicated and time consuming. It is usually not worthwhile. However, if you feel that you must appeal your case it would be a good idea to consult a lawyer or paralegal to help you. Lawyers often use other lawyers who specialize in handling appeals and so should you. The following will show you what is involved and give you an idea of how to proceed.

An appeal is the process of having the decision of the trial court reviewed by a higher court. This court may be called a "Court of Appeal" or an "Appellate Department" or some other name. There are usually three judges who sit on this type of court. It takes a majority to rule either for or against the person appealing. The "appellant" is the person who brings the appeal to the court. The "respondent" is the person who responds or answers the appeal. The defendant is usually the "appellant" in a traffic situation and the prosecution is usually the "respondent". However, the roles could be reversed. The prosecution cannot appeal from a verdict of not guilty.

You have a right to appeal from a verdict of guilty after judgment (sentence) has been pronounced. You may also appeal from the sentence.

It is very important to remember that the Appellate Court will almost never reverse (find against) a decision of the trial court which was made on a factual basis. This means that if your complaint is that the judge believed the officer instead of you and/or your witnesses you lose. The only instance where such a reversal takes place is if the record shows that there was no evidence to support the prosecution's case. This is extremely rare.

The appellate court will only, other than mentioned above, consider legal errors by the court which had an effect on your case. If the trial court made an error and it did not harm your case ("harmless error") than the appellate court will not overturn the trial court's decision. If the error was such that you otherwise would have been entitled to a finding of not guilty or a dismissal of your case ("prejudicial error"), you may get a reversal of the finding of the trial court.

An example of "prejudicial error" would be the judge refusing to allow you to make a closing statement to argue your case. An example of "harmless error" would be the judge overruling a hearsay objection where the evidence had already been allowed into evidence.

You are entitled to be represented by an attorney during an appeal in the same manner as you were entitled during the proceedings in the trial court. That is, if you were entitled to appointed counsel you will be entitled to appointed counsel in the appellate court. However, you must usually file papers declaring that you are indigent and request appointed counsel in the appellate court at the same time that you file your notice of appeal. These papers are usually obtainable from the higher court. Otherwise you must hire your own attorney or represent yourself.

The appellate courts are usually pretty forgiving of lapses in the exact formalities required in an appeal if you are representing yourself *in propria personae* or "pro per" as it is commonly referred to. However, they don't have to be and can indeed not consider your appeal because you haven't complied with the rules. It is, therefore, important to find out what the rules are in your particular jurisdiction.

The rules are usually published under a title called "Rules of Court". You must check with your local court or legal library to find them and find out what you are supposed to do. Also, there will be form books and books on procedure in the legal library which will give explicit directions on what to do. (See APPENDIX B—Law Books.) It is a good idea to look these items over and adapt them to your case. This is what lawyers will do in most cases before they make up a brand new form. Of course they will also use their own form files which have been developed over the years.

This technique is easy to say but hard to do. The law librarian will only be able to show you the form books. She will not be able or allowed to tell you how to use them as that would be practicing law without a license. You will have to figure it out yourself or hire a lawyer which is strongly recommended.

The "Rules of Court" will also tell you what kind of paper to use and how many copies of your document are to be provided. There is a trend for 8 1/2 by 11 inch legal paper to replace the older 8 1/2 by 13 or 14 inch legal paper that had been customary. This legal paper is numbered so that each line has a number and can be referred to by page and line number. (See Figures 11 and 13.)

Procedures vary but the following is an example of the steps required in a misdemeanor appeal which is the same as a infraction appeal in California.

•Notice of Appeal:

This one page form must be filed with the clerk

of the court within thirty days of your being sentenced. Once that document is filed, the court is required to stay the execution of your sentence; that is, you do not have to do your sentence until and unless you lose your appeal. If you are in jail you are entitled to bail on appeal. This may not do you much good if you cannot raise the money but you are entitled to it.

•Proposed Settled Statement on Appeal:

This document must be filed within fifteen days of the filing of the Notice of Appeal. This document must set forth your grounds for appeal such as: denial of your motion to dismiss for lack of speedy trial, denial of a motion to move the case to the county seat, denial of your right to cross-examine witnesses, etc.. You must set forth a factual summary of the proceedings in question. If the proceedings were recorded either by court reporter or by tape recording you should request that the factual statement of the Settled Statement should be a transcript of the proceedings. Note that if you are not indigent you may have to pay for your copy of the transcript. If you are indigent you should say so when requesting that the transcript be made a part of the record so that you do not have to pay for it. You should always find out if a court reporter or recorder is used before proceeding with the trial so that you can request that a court reporter be present or a tape recording be made of the proceedings.

If there was no transcript or the judge refuses to allow its use, you must prepare a written statement of the facts that were actually presented as evidence by both sides—Not what you wish had been presented.

Once you have prepared the Proposed Settled Statement, you must have it served either in person by someone other than yourself or by mail on the prosecuting attorney and the court. The server of the Proposed Settled Statement will sign a document, under "Penalty of Perjury" entitled "Proof of Service" certifying that he is over eighteen, not a party to the action and that he served the document on the prosecuting attorney at such address in person (in which case there will be a place where the representative of the prosecutor should sign showing receipt) or by mailing it to the prosecutor at a given address on the date mailed. This declaration is attached to the Proposed Settled Statement which is served on the court. It may also be mailed to the court clerk or served personally. In person service is always best because you can verify that the various documents were actually received.

•Proposed Settled Statement by Prosecution:

This document will be prepared by the prosecution if they disagree with your Proposed Settled Statement. It must be prepared by a lawyer, not the police officer. Remember when you are "pro per" you are a lawyer.

•Settlement Conference:

This hearing is set before the trial judge and should be attended by you and the prosecution. There will usually be a discussion as to what the "Settled Statement" should contain based upon the submitted "Proposed Settled Statements". Once an agreement has been reached as to the final statement you will be responsible for preparing it. It is important to remember that what is decided here is what the Appellate Court will base their decision on. So be firm in arguing that your statement is accurate and should prevail. The final decision is up to the judge.

•The Settled Statement On Appeal is also called

an Engrossed Statement.

The appealing party is responsible for preparing this document for signature by the judge. It will be the same as the Proposed Settled Statement except for the title ("Proposed" is dropped). It should reflect exactly what was decided at the Settlement Conference. There should be a place for the judge to sign certifying it as correct. It should be served as above on the prosecution and then served on the court with the proof of service. This must be filed within five days of the conference.

•Transfer to the Appellate Court:

Once all the papers and records are put together the entire case is transferred to the Appellate Court. You will be notified. The notice will include a new appeals case number which should be used on everything submitted thereafter to the appellate department.

•Opening Brief:

This document must be filed within twenty days of the date of transfer from the trial court. This date will be on the notice of transfer. This document contains your arguments as to why your case was prejudiced by the rulings of the trial court. The opening brief is usually in four parts, as follows, although this format is not required,

1. Statement of Facts: A two or three paragraph summary of the facts of the case. You refer to details by the page and line number of the Settled Statement or transcript so the appellate judges can refer to those documents.

2. Issues: This is a list of issues in the form of questions which raise each legal issue you are going to cover.

3. Summary of Argument: This is a summary

of the full detailed legal argument which will follow.

4. Argument: This is the main part of the brief. Each point is listed under the proper heading and contains a statement of the appropriate law and where it is found (code section) or case law and its location (citation). Be brief, but thorough. Present each point in a logical manner and close with a conclusion which brings all the points together.

One original, a copy to the prosecution, a copy for each judge of the appellate court, and one for your file are prepared.

A copy of the brief is served on the prosecution, and the trial court. Then the original and three copies are filed with the appellate court with proof of service attached to the original as mentioned above. When you file these papers you should have the clerk of the appellate court stamp your copy with a "file stamp" which will state "FILED" and the date. It is important that you keep this copy as you will be referring to it later.

This is a total of six copies and one original.

•Respondent's Brief: This is a brief similar to your brief in which the respondent (prosecution) will answer the points raised in your brief. This also has to be filed within twenty days of the date of transfer and a copy sent to you.

•Reply Brief: This is optional. If after reading the Respondent's Brief you wish to answer any specific points you may do so limiting yourself to the new point or arguments only. This has to be filed within ten days after the brief of the respondent is filed. You make the same number of copies and serve them as before, except you do not have to serve the Reply Brief on the appellate court.

•Hearing: The hearing will be months after you start the procedure. You will be notified by mail of the date, time and place. At the hearing you and a prosecutor, usually not the trial prosecutor, will be permitted to present arguments and answer any questions the appellate judges may have. They may already have decided the case based on the briefs and if so there will be no argument. If you are questioned just answer the question. The judges will either make a decision then or take it "under advisement" meaning that you will be notified by mail.

•Remittitur: This is the decision of the court. If "Affirmed" you lose. This means that they agree with the trial court and must start or complete your sentence. You will usually just get a postcard with that statement on it. This is called "postcarding".

If "Reversed" you win. The appellate court may order the case dismissed, returned to the trial court for a new trial or sentence or other directions. They may have a written decision explaining their reasons. If dismissed your fine will be refunded and the conviction will be removed from your driving record. But if you have done any jail time you will just have to write that off as you will not be compensated for it.

If you are granted a new trial, you are entitled to have it within the statutory time for trial as from the date of arraignment either thirty or forty-five days. If it is not set by the trial court within that time you will be entitled to a dismissal.

As you can see from the above, an appeal is quite complicated, demanding and time consuming. More so in fact than a trial. If you decide to appeal your case research the law thoroughly. Try to write clearly and to the point. Separate each point and support each part of your argument with as much law as you find that is to the point. There are good books available in your law library which will assist you in this process. It is not easy. Some lawyers specialize in doing appeals which are referred to them by other lawyers or the court.

It is strongly recommended that you use the services of an attorney. However, a person representing himself can handle such a appeal. But be careful to follow the rules and be especially careful to file the notices and papers within the time limits specified by your jurisdiction.

1	<u>DECLARATION OF SERVICE BY MAIL</u>
2	
3	The undersigned declares under penalty of
4	perjury that the following is true and correct:
5	I am a citizen of the United States, over
6	eighteen years of age, not a party to the within
7	cause and am employed by_____in
8	the County of_____.
9	On the date of execution hereof, I served the
10	following:
11	(insert name of document)
12	
13	by depositing a true copy thereof, enclosed in a
14	sealed envelope, with proper postage affixed, ad-
15	dressed as follows:
16	
17	
18	
19	Executed this____day of_____,19___.
20	_____
21	(type name)
22	

PROOF OF SERVICE

FIGURE 14

GLOSSARY

Acquittal: Not guilty. A motion requesting that the judge make a finding of not guilty before the defense case is put on.

Admonishment: A motion which has the judge tell the witnesses not to discuss the case.

Affidavit of Prejudice: An oral or written statement that a particular judge is prejudiced against you and should not hear your case.

Affidavit for Cause: A written statement similar to an Affidavit of Prejudice except that it states the exact reasons for the belief that the judge is prejudiced.

Annotations: The notes of decisions of cases which interpret a specific law.

Appeal: A request to a higher court to reconsider the decision of the trial court.

Appellant: The party who takes an appeal from one court to another. The defendant, if he is the one who appeals.

Arraignment: The first appearance in court where the charges are read and a plea entered.

Bail: The amount of money needed to get released from jail.

Bail bond (bond): A bond which is posted to get you out of jail. It is a guarantee that if you do not return to court the person posting the bond will pay the bail money.

Bailiff: Law enforcement officer whose job is to enforce order in the court.

Bar: The railing separating the audience from the courtroom. Also the organization to which lawyers belong.

Bench warrant: A warrant of arrest issued by the judge for a failure to appear, obey a subpoena, pay a fine, do charitable work or comply with any other court order.

Blood Alcohol Content (BAC): The quantity of alcohol in the blood. Usually given in percent. 0.10% BAC is considered under the influence in most states.

Certified Copy: A copy of a document that has been

stamped with a seal indicating that it is a true and correct copy and that the copy has been made by a authorized person.

Citation (traffic ticket): A statement of the charge against you and a notice to appear. A release without bail.

Cite: The reference to a legal authority. This is done by giving the name of the authority, date, and where (in which books) it can be found.

Challenge for Cause: A challenge to a juror for which some cause or reason is alleged. For example, that the juror is prejudiced.

Challenge, Peremptory: A challenge to a juror for which no cause need be given. Usually limited in number depending on the kind of case.

Commissioner: A person, usually a lawyer, who is appointed by the judge or judges of a court to sit as a judge and who may hear cases if everyone so agrees.

Conclusion: An objection that the witness is making a conclusion rather than testifying to what he saw.

Confrontation: The right to have the witnesses against you in court for your trial.

Contempt of Court: Any act which is calculated to embarrass, hinder or obstruct the court or lessen its dignity or authority.

Continuance: A motion to continue the case to a different date.

Court: Refers to the courthouse and the courtroom as well as the judicial officers.

Court Clerk: Keeps the official record of the proceedings in court and much more.

Court Trial: Trial in which only the judge hears the evidence and gives a verdict.

Cross-examination: The questioning of witnesses by the opposing side.

Direct examination: The questioning of witnesses by the side calling the witnesses.

Exclude witnesses: A motion which requests the judge to order the witnesses to wait outside the courtroom.

Expungement: A means of having a conviction removed from the record or minimizing its effects.

Felony: A crime which carries with it a state prison sentence.

Foundation, Lack of: An objection that there has been insufficient evidence to allow the witness to testify.

Forfeiture: The giving up of the bail bond or the bail on a failure to appear. In traffic cases a forfeiture will be treated as a guilty plea and the money, if posted in full, may be used as the fine thus ending the proceeding.

Furtive gesture: A surreptitious movement made by a suspect seen by a police officer who feels that the person is hiding something.

Guilty: A plea which admits the charge and allows the judge to sentence.

Guilty with explanation: Not a legal plea, but it is treated as a guilty plea which indicates you wish to tell the judge a reason for your actions.

Hearing officer: Same as referee.

Hearsay: An objection to a question calling for testimony of what some person not present in court said in order to prove the fact in question.

Indigent: Not having enough money to afford a attorney or to pay a fine.

Infraction: A crime which carries a penalty of only a fine and no jail. See also petty misdemeanors.

Judge: A person, usually a lawyer, who is appointed by the governor of the state or the President of the U.S. or is elected to decide cases and impose sentences.

Judge Pro Tempore (pro tem): One appointed for a time during which he acts as a judge.

Judgment: The official decision of the court. Also used to mean the sentence of the court in criminal law.

Jury Trial: A trial in which a group of your peers, usually 6 to 12 in number, hear the evidence and decide the case.

Leading Question: Putting the words in the witness' mouth.

Magistrate: Judge.

Misdemeanor: A crime which carries a maximum county jail penalty, except for petty misdemeanors which only carry a fine.—See Infraction.

Motion: The formal manner of submitted a request to the court.

No Contest (Nolo contendere): I will not contest it. Treated the same as a guilty plea in allowing the judge to sentence. May not be used to prove the case in a civil proceeding.

Not Guilty: A plea which denies the charge and sets into motion the trial process.

Nystagmus: An involuntary rapid movement of the eyeball. It may be horizontal or vertical or rotary. Believed to be a symptom of intoxication.

Objection: A statement by a party that he objects or disagrees with some matter during a trial or proceeding.

Ordinance: Laws enacted by a local community as opposed to statutes which are enacted by the state.

Own Recognizance (OR): Release from custody on your promise to come to court without the necessity of posting bail or bond.

Pacing: Measuring speed by matching speed of patrol car with other vehicle.

Perjury: Lying under oath.

Plea bargain: A deal made between the prosecution and the defendant as to either a reduction in charge or fine.

Penalty Assessment: A sum of money added to a fine.

Point Count: Numbers given to each conviction of a moving violation which added together can result in suspension of the driving privilege.

Prima Facie Speed: The speed which is considered safe for the road conditions, time of day and weather.

Prior: A prior conviction of a specific crime which is used to increase the penalties of a new offense.

Probable Cause: A reasonable belief in the existence of facts which would lead a reasonable person to believe that the accused had committed a crime.

Probation: Allowing a person convicted of an offense to be released under a suspension of sentence during a period of good behavior and under specified conditions.

Probation, Summary: Probation without supervision.

Probation, Formal: Probation which is supervised by a probation officer.

Pro per (In propria persona): In one's own proper person or self-representation.

Prosecutor: Attorney representing the "people": i.e., state, county, or city.

Public Defender: Attorney who represents those without money in criminal cases, except ordinary traffic tickets.

Radar: A means of measuring speed by bouncing electronic signals off of your vehicle and measuring how fast they return.

Rap sheet: A listing of a individual's criminal record.

Recess: A break in the court proceedings.

Referee: A person, usually a lawyer, who is appointed temporarily to sit as a judge; similar to a commissioner.

Reinstatement of license: This is required after the period of suspension or revocation of one's driving privilege has passed before one can legally drive.

Remittitur: The returning of the record by a court of appeal after its decision to the court from which it came along with the decision of the court of appeal.

Respondent: The party who contends against an appeal. This would be the prosecution if the defendant appeals.

Rest: The ending of presentation of evidence by one party.

Second call: The second time the judge calls your case to see if your are there and ready. If you do not answer he will order a bench warrant.

Speculation: An objection that the witness is guessing in reaching some conclusion or statement of fact.

Speed Trap: Wherein an officer measures speed by timing the car's movement over a measured distance.

Stipulation: An agreement between the parties.

Subpoena: A court order requiring the appearance of the person who is given the subpoena.

Subpoena Dueces Tecum (SDT): A court order for the production in court of material things as opposed to people.

Traffic School: A place where you can go for traffic education and avoid a conviction or addition to a point count.

Traffic Clerk: Sends the traffic cases into the courtroom, accepts bail and fine money and may be able to set court appearances and grant an extension to a fine.

Transcript: A copy of the official record of the court proceedings if taken down by a court reporter or electronic recording.

Voir dire (to speak the truth): The questioning of prospective jurors to determine if you wish to have them on your jury. Also to question a witness regarding his expertise or competency.

VASCAR: Visual Average Speed Computer and Recorder. Essentially a timer connected to a computer to calculate speed.

INDEX

ORDER FORM

Allenby Press
701 S. First Ave. Ste.272a
Arcadia, CA 91006
(818) 446-6700

Please send me_____copies of
TRAFFIC COURT-"How To Win" @ $12.95 per book.
I understand that I may return the book for a full refund if not satis-
fied.

Name:_____

Address:_____

City:_____State:____Zip:_____

Californians: Please add 78¢ sales tax per book.

Shipping: $1.50 for the first book and 75¢ for each additional
book

___I can't wait 3-4 weeks for Book Rate. Here is $3 per book for Air
Mail.

TOTAL ENCLOSED:_____.

- -

ORDER FORM

Allenby Press
701 S. First Ave. Ste.272a
Arcadia, CA 91006
(818) 446-6700

Please send me_____copies of
TRAFFIC COURT-"How To Win" @ $12.95 per book.
I understand that I may return the book for a full refund if not satis-
fied.

Name:_____

Address:_____

City:_____State:____Zip:_____

Californians: Please add 78¢ sales tax per book.

Shipping: $1.50 for the first book and 75¢ for each additional
book

___I can't wait 3-4 weeks for Book Rate. Here is $3 per book for Air
Mail.

TOTAL ENCLOSED:_____.